The Marketing Dictionary

Compiled and edited by
Adam Starchild

International Law & Taxation Publishers
London

The Marketing Dictionary

Compiled and edited by
Adam Starchild

ISBN 1-893713-15-6

International Law & Taxation Publishers
London
http://www.internationallawandtaxationpublishers.com

Absentee Management — A condition that exists when executives of a large corporation have their offices in one city whereas their operation divisions are scattered throughout the country.

Accelerated Fashion Change—Stepped-up chances dictated by fashion leaders and manufacturers where fashion obsolescence plays increasing importance.

Accessories—Women's fashion apparel worn with dresses, coats, suits. Sportswear; includes fine and costume jewelry, neckwear, scarfs, handbags, and small leather goods, millinery, gloves, hosiery, shoes, handkerchief, watches, artificial flowers ribbons.

Accessory Items—Merchandise that "goes with" or is coordinated with larger items.

Accommodation Desk—A centrally located fixture in a smaller store where calls, gift wrapping, and other services are performed for customer convenience.

Account—A bookkeeping record of a commercial transaction. A customer or client of a business who buys on time and pays according to some prearranged credit plan.

Account Assets—The various things owned by a business enterprise such as cash, stock-in-trade, supplies, machinery, furniture, fixtures and land.

Account Capital—The net worth, the capital investment, or the owner's equity. In accounting the term is often used to mean fixed assets as a class.

Account, Open-book—The seller's accounting record of an unsecured sale of merchandise. A retail charge account.

The Marketing Dictionary

Accountability—Being obligated to stand behind performance. The obligation of a subordinate to report to a superior on the way a dedicated job has been performed.

Accounting—The recording, classifying, and summarization of business transactions, and interpreting this compiled information.

Accounts Payable—A current liability representing the amount owned by an individual or a business to a creditor for merchandise or services purchased on open account or short term credit.

Accounts Receivable—Money owed a business enterprise for merchandise bought on open account (i.e., without the giving of a note or other evidence of debt.)

Accounts Slow Pay and Unsatisfactory—Accounts receivable which have not been paid as agreed or in accordance with credit terms.

Accrued Expense—An account on an income statement indicating earnings which have not yet been received.

Additional Markup—An increase in price above the original retail price.

Additional Markup Cancellation—A decrease in retail price from a point above original retail to original retail.

Adjustment Letter—A letter sent by a business making an adjustment to a customer who was not satisfied with a transaction.

Administered Prices—When a seller, usually a producer, establishes his prices at a predetermined level.

Administrative Advertising Director—Responsible for preparation of sales promotion budgets including allocation by months to various media including cooperative funds from resources, plus staff and freelance compensation; and for maintenance of budgets by months. In medium- and smaller-sized stores these functions are generally performed by the sales promotion or advertising manager.

Administrative Management—Same as Top Management.

Advance Dating—Dating which is some time after actual shipment, giving additional time in which payment may be made and cash discount deducted. The time for payment of the invoice is computed from the advance dating, rather than from the invoice date.

Advertising—Any paid-for form of non-personal presentation of goods, services, or ideas to a group.

Advertising Agency—An organization which prepares and places advertisements for circulation in various types of media to promote the distribution and sale of products for clients.

Advertising Allowance—The portion of cost the manufacturer bears toward the promotion and advertising of his product at the wholesale or retail level. The amount of advertising expense for which a wholesaler or retailer is reimbursed by the manufacturer.

Advertising, Black and White—A space advertisement that appears with black print on white paper as distinguished from an advertisement which employs colors.

Advertising Campaign—A series of advertisements, using a definite theme of appeal planned to accomplish a specific task.

Advertising Color—Any paid form of advertising which uses color as an integral part of the presentation.

Advertising, Commodity—That form of advertising which is designed to point up the virtues, or call attention to, a specific commodity or group of commodities.

The Marketing Dictionary

Advertising Council—Dedicated to the idea that advertising could and should be used in the public interest as it had been in the private interest. Organized in 1941.

Advertising, Direct Mail—Any kind of advertising that goes directly to the prospective buyer through the mails, including letters, booklets, samples, folders, and leaflets.

Advertising Folder—A pamphlet, brochure, or folded paper on which a printed advertisement appears.

Advertising, Institutional—Advertising which seeks to build goodwill with the consuming public or with people of a business organization.

Advertising Manager—Normally supervises all printed and broadcast medial.

Advertising, Point of Purchase—Advertising designed to attract the consumer public in retail stores at the place where the product is bought.

Advertising, Public Relations—Advertising such as institutional advertising designed to gain the goodwill of various publics, such as stockholders, suppliers, employees, and consumers of a business firm.

Advertising, Remembrance—Advertising placed in media of a long lasting nature, such as calendars, novelties, playing cards, and leather goods, designed to serve as a reminder to selected audiences of the name, the products and the location of the business.

Advertising Specialties—Consists of a large number of different items that are useful in carrying an advertiser's name or a brief sales message. [See: Advertising, Remembrance].

Affidavit—A written statement of testimony made before a notary public or other person authorized by law to administer an oath or affirmation.

agate Line—Newspaper advertising unit of measurement; an agate line is one column wide by 1/14th of an inch deep.

Agency—A business relationship between two parties whereby one party, the principal, delegates certain powers to the other party, the agent.

Agent—A person who acts on behalf of another person, his principal, in conducting transactions with a third person.

Agent Middleman—A middleman who negotiates purchase or sales or both but who does not take title to goods.

Alien Corporation—A company doing business within the United States that has been organized in another country.

Allocated Expenses—Expenses, other than direct, for which good and appropriate bases of expense distribution exists, so that the assignment of expense represents a reasonable estimate of true expense incurred by each department.

Allowance—A credit in lieu of a cash refund given to a customer who is not satisfied with a business transaction.

Allowances from Vendors—The rebates and credits granted by manufacturers and wholesalers on purchases made by the store. They may reflect defects in merchandise, substitutions, declines in wholesale prices, and payments for promotional services to be performed by the retailer.

Allowances to Customers—Price reductions resulting in refunds to customers after the original sales where made.

Alteration Costs- The costs incurred in altering and finishing merchandise to meed the needs of customers at the time of sale.

The Marketing Dictionary

Amortize—To provide a fund for the payment of a long-term loan or bond by setting aside an amount of money periodically. It is also used to mean writing off the cost of a machine over a period of years.

Annual Report—A report issued by a corporation, covering the previous year's activities, financial statement and future prospects.

Annuity—A form of an insurance which in return for an agreed-on premium, provides the insured a regular income immediately or after he reaches a specified age.

Anticipation—An extra discount commonly allowed by vendors when a bill is paid before the expiration of the case discount period. It is usually figured at the rate of 5% per annum. However, some vendors specifically state on their invoices that no anticipation is allowed and in such cases there is no advantage in prepaying the bill.

Antiquated—Where a store's physical plant needs renovating or perhaps entire rebuilding and refixturing.

Appraisal—An evaluation of property such as real estate, made by a person authorized to do so.

Arrears—An obligation which remains unpaid beyond the date of maturity.

Assets—Everything a corporation owns or due to it: cash, investments, money due it, materials and inventories, which are called current asses; buildings and machinery, which are known as fixed assets; and patents and goodwill, called intangible assets.

Assets, Current—Cash and other assets readily converted into cash, such as accounts and notes receivable, inventory and prepaid expenses.

Assets, Fixed—A term used in a balance sheet to denote assets of a lasting nature that can be used repeatedly such as building or machinery.

Assets, Frozen—Assets which cannot be readily converted into cash.

Assets, Intangible—Assets, such as goodwill, patents and organization costs, grouped under the caption "intangibles" in a model balance sheet.

Assistant Buyer—Responsible for department's merchandise operation when buyer is in market; fulling merchandise in receiving and marketing department; follow-through on advertising details and okaying copy, illustrations from merchandise viewpoint.

Assortment Plan—Complete range of merchandise in a category planned to various depths of inventory to meet customer demand.

At the Market—An order to buy or sell a security "at the market" means it will be bought or sold by the floor broker at the best available price when the order reaches the floor.

Auction Company—Sell at wholesale by the auction method. Sales are conducted under definite rules and are usually made to the highest bidder.

Audience—In advertising this refers to the readers, listeners, or viewers of an advertising message.

Audited Sales—Resulting net figures of the sales for a period, daily, weekly, monthly, semi-annually, or annually.

Auditing Department—Department in the controller's division whose responsibility is the daily auditing of sales and return-merchandise transactions.

Authorizing—Approval of a charge transaction by credit personnel when the amount of the sale exceeds floor limits or when identification of the customer and account is required.

The Marketing Dictionary

Automatic Basement—Basement or downstairs store in a large department store where prices of merchandise are automatically marked down after a specific period of time has elapsed.

Automatic Reorder—Reordering staple merchandise on the basis of a predetermined minimum quantity; when this minimum is reached, the quantity of the initial order is again purchased.

Autonomous Operation—Achieved by branch stores as they grow larger, develop more autonomy in operation, and are treated on "equal stores" basis with downtown store.

Average Gross Sale—Dollar amount of gross sales divided by number of sales transactions or sales checks which produced the gross sales.

Average Stock (same as average inventory)—An average of the stock on hand at representative dates throughout the year or season.

Averaging Markup—Adjusting the proportions of goods purchased at varying markups in order to achieve a desired aggregate markup either for a certain period of on an individual lot.

Profitable merchandising often leads management to seek out opportunities to increase the average markup by increasing the proportion of high-markup goods, but in some lines completion is forcing lower average markups which may increase profits if sales can be materially increased.

Backlog—A reserve or accumulation of unfilled orders.

Back Order—The portion of a customer's order undelivered for any reason, but usually because of the unavailability of product or merchandise.

Backup Stock—Additional merchandise available in warehouse or in forward stockroom. Particularly important for runners or best selling staples.

Bad Dept—A debt which is uncollectible.

Bailment—The act of an owner of goods turning them over to another for repair, storage, rental, safekeeping, or the like.

Balance-and-Mix—A complete assortment; in rugs includes accent rugs, broadloom rugs, scatter rugs, orientals, remnants to satisfy wants, needs, pocket books of majority of customers.

Balanced stock—Balanced stock and/or assortment makes available what the customers want throughout all price zones or price ranges in proportion to that demand.

Balance Sheet—Lists the assets, the liabilities, and the proprietorship interest of the owners of a business.

Bargain Basement—The basement of downstairs store of a department store that specializes in price lines that upstairs store does not carry or of which the upstairs store duplicates only the top price line; the downstairs store emphasizes special values.

Bargain Store—Where everything is stocked provided it can be sold in quantity at a sub-market price. Distress merchandise and job lots are often bought in huge quantities, but little or no attempt, made to maintain stock assortment.

Barter—The exchange of goods without money.

Basic Assortment—The smallest number of pieces within a grouping of merchandise to provide sufficient sizes, colors, style numbers, etc., to satisfy customer demand.

Basic Stocks—Items, numbers, or models that must be included in a line or classification. A basic stock is primarily an assortment of the bread-and-butter items that enjoy day-to-day customer demand. Basic stock is usually staples but non-staple items become basic when for fashion or fad reasons, they enjoy temporarily increased customer demand. The best rule for basic stock is having what the customer wants when she wants it.

Bear—A person who believes stock prices will go down; a "bear market" is a market of declining prices.

Best Buy—An item carried in a price line that is a best buy from the angle of the customer who is interested in intrinsic quality.

Best-Seller or Runner—Seasonal or year-round item or number in a line that sells throughout season or year at full markon, that merits continuous promotion in displays, advertising, suggestive selling.

Better Business Bureau—Financed by local media and business interests for purpose of promoting accuracy and honesty in advertising and selling.

Bid—The price offered by those wishing to buy given stocks or bonds. Also, the price the dealer will pay for securities of the investor. Also, the prices offered in competitive bidding by financial houses competing for a new security issue. Also, a competitive off in order to get a contract to do work.

Bid Board—A name given to the New York Stock Exchange.

Big Ticket—Usually big in physical size and size of price. Natural habitat: major appliances, furniture, and other hard goods. Often uses tick-toe system of crossing through squares when it is sold for read-and-run stock inventory.

Billed Cost—The invoice cost of purchases less trade and quantity discounts but without the dedication of cash discount.

Biller—Personnel in the accounts receivable department whose responsibility is to prepare a bill for the customer for purchases made during the preceding month.

Billing—The act of sending a bill or a notice to a person or firm owing money. The procedure of sending a statement of what is due and payable by a business firm who sold or delivered goods or services under some agreed-upon credit arrangement.

Billing Cycle—A system of billing whereby a company will mail out a certain number of statements each day or at periodic intervals during the month in order to balance the workload for this kind of work.

Bill of Sale—A written agreement by the terms of which the title or other interest of one person in goods is transferred or assigned to another.

Bill of Lading—Form used by the carrier denoting the consignor, consignee, number and weight of packages, description, shipping charges (sometimes, not always), date, and other information necessary for shipment and receipt of goods into the store.

Bills of Exchange—Drafts used in domestic trade, except that they may be written in terms of francs or marks instead of dollars.

Blank-Check Buying—A retailer places an open order with a vendor generally to start off a season, with specific details following through season as needed.

Blanket Order—Pre-season order to meet anticipated needs, placed before production has started; buyer orders against blanket order to meet needs as season arrives and progresses.

Blind Advertisement—An advertisement which does not have a company name or signature on it. A common example is a help-wanted advertisement in the classified section of a newspaper, describing the position but not naming the company involved.

The Marketing Dictionary

Blind Products—Unusual, interesting, intriguing items producing a higher-than-normal markon because of special appeal to customers.

Block Style—A form of business letter in which there is no indentation made for the opening line of a paragraph.

Blue Chip—Common stock in a company known nationally for the quality and wide acceptance of its products or services, and for its ability to make money and pay dividends in good times and bad. Usually such stocks are relatively high-priced and offer relatively low yields.

Board of Directors—A group of people elected by the shareowners of a corporation. The board makes policy decisions and selects officers to run the company.

Bond—A bond is basically an IOU. The person who invests his money in a bond is lending a company or government a sum of money for a specified time, with the understanding that the borrower will pay it back and pay interest for using it.

Bond Averages—Computed daily similar to stocks. Dow-Jones bond averages are the best known type.

Bond Discount—The amount by which the price on a bond averages are the best known type.

Bond Discount—The amount by which the price on a bond is less than the stated value of the bond.

Bond Premium—Amount by which the price exceeds the stated value on a bond.

Bonus (P.M. Premium Money)—Additional bonus raid to salespeople for selling slow-moving, pre-season, or higher-priced merchandise, or for a special promotion; sometimes paid by vendor upon approval by store.

Book Inventory—An inventory which is not the result of actual stocktaking but of adding the units and the cost of incoming goods to previous inventory figures and deducting the units and costs of outgoing goods.

Boutique—Small shop; especially one that sells fashionable clothes and accessories for women.

Boycott—Takes place when union members refuse to purchase products from companies whose employees are on strike or where some condition prevails to which the union is opposed.

Branch House—An establishment maintained by a manufacturer or a wholesaler, detached from the headquarters establishment and used primarily for the purpose of carrying stocks, selling, and delivering his product.

Branch Merchandising Plan—Increasing influence of branch store managers and their merchandising staffs in recommending or requesting items, lines, or brands from specific resources.

Branch Store—Owned and operated by the parent or flagship store; generally located in a suburban area under the name of the flagship store.

Brand—Is a word, letter or group of words or letters comprising a name or design or a combination of these which identifies the goods or services of one seller and/or distinguishes them from those of competitors. Brand is a more inclusive general term than trademark.

Brand Name—A brand or part of a brand consisting of a word, letter, or group of words or letters comprising a name which identifies the goods or services of a seller or grouping of sellers and distinguishes them from those of competitors.

Brand, National—The name of a product which is sold throughout the country as distinguished from a private brand.

The Marketing Dictionary

Brand, Private—A product name used specifically by an individual firm.

Breach of Promise—The failure to perform a duty which has been agreed upon by contract.

Break-Even Chart—A chart used in budgetary control on which the break-even point is shown and which presents relationships between volume, costs, prices and profit.

Break-Even Cost—The cost price of an article for which the retail price has been determined that will provide a markup just sufficient to cover the direct expenses incurred, or probably to be incurred, by stocking and selling the item.

Break-Even Point—The level in sales volume at which a company's revenue equals its overhead and variable costs.

Break-Even Retail—A retail price that will provide a markup just sufficient to cover the direct expenses incurred, or probably to be incurred, in stocking and selling the item. It is the price at which the item is expected to contribute neither to profit nor to loss; that is, it provides no controllable margin to help pay for the joint expenses of either the department or the store.

Bridal Advisor—Responsible for bridal bureau and, in some stores, responsible for the bridal salon where wedding gowns and fashion accessories are sold.

Bridal Consultant—Generally located in bridal salon to help bride in selection of gown, accessories, intimate apparel, brides maids costumes; frequently goes to the bride's home to arrange wedding gifts, to the church to supervise wedding preparations.

Bridal Registry—Registration bureau, preferably located in or near china, glassware, or bride-to-be in selection of patterns, then registers patterns and maintains record of what pieces have been purchased by relatives, friends, and guests to avoid duplication of gifts.

Broker—An agent, often a member of a Stock Exchange firm or an Exchange member himself, who handles the public's orders to buy and sell securities.

Brokerage Firm—A group of brokers who buy and sell for their customers, and also assist in financing these transactions.

Brown Goods—Radios, television, electronics.

Budget—A target, insofar as plans income and expenditures are concerned, agreed upon by the management of a company as a measure of good performance during a specified future period.

Budget, Advertising—That portion of the budget of a business which concerns itself with the plans and anticipated expenditures for advertising.

Budget, Sales—That portion of the budget of a business which is concerned with plans and anticipated expenditures for sales.

Budget Store—May be a section of flagship store or branch store specializing in price lines the regular upstairs store does not carry or of which the upstairs store duplicates only the top price lines; may also be called Bargain Basement or Downstairs Store.

Bulk Merchandise Delivery—Large merchandise items such as major appliances, furniture, bedding, and rugs requiring at least two men to deliver, that cannot be handled by parcel delivery men. Some stores employ commercial trucking companies, or manufacturer's distributor delivers directly to store's customer.

Bull—A person who believes stock prices will rise; a "bull market" is one with rising prices [See Bear]

The Marketing Dictionary

Business Communications—The various forms of oral and written messages used by a business in the conduct of its affairs.

Business Conditions—Any circumstances or external factors which modify the nature, existence or occurrence of business activities. The environment in which business operates at any particular point in time.

Business Cycle—A recurring sequence of changes in business activity. Following a period of prosperity, business activity declines through a recession to a low point, called a depression. A period of recovery then follows when business becomes more and more active until prosperity is restored and the cycle is complete.

Business Law—The same as commercial law.

Business Papers—Trade, industrial, and professional magazines and newspapers that circulate only among businessmen and that are useful in advertising industrial or business goods and services.

Buyer—A consumer. Also an employee whose work is to buy goods for a business firm.

Buyer's Market—Market situation in which manufacturer's inventories are high and demand is slow; also known as a "soft" market.

Buying by Specifications—Where store submits definite specifications to manufacturer, rather than selecting from goods already on the market. Private or controlled brands are normally purchased by an individual store or through a regional buying office on specifications.

Buying Committee—Composed of the top marketing and purchasing personnel in the company concerned, is charged with the duty of determining the acceptability of new items that are offered to their stores for sale.

Buying, Forward—A policy of purchasing in large amounts at infrequent intervals as distinguished from hand-to-mouth buying.

Buying Group (Buying Office, Resident Buying Office)—Organization representing group of non-competing stores, formed primarily for buying merchandise; may be independent, store-owned, or own the stores.

Buying Habits—The observable way that buyers or consumers behave when purchasing goods and services.

Buying Hours—Specific hours set up by store or regional buying offices for buyers to meet with vendor salesmen and inspect merchandise samples.

Buying Power—The value of a specified monetary unit in terms of the amount of commodities or services that can be bought with it. Also, the expendable income of a specific group or class of purchasers.

Buying, Reciprocal—The act of purchasing from vendors who are customers as distinguished from vendors who are not customers.

Bylaw—Rules and regulations a board of directors is to follow in conducting the business.

By-Product—A product resulting as an incident of the manufacture of some other product. In the production of lignite coal, for example, some of the by-products are coal tar and ammonia salts.

Calendar Week—A week beginning at 12:01 A.M. Sunday and ending at 12:00 P.M. Saturday.

Callable Bonds—Bonds which have the feature of a call price.

Call Credit—Used when merchandise is picked up by store's delivery system from a customer, returned to store, and customer is credited for price of merchandise.

Call Price—The exact amount at which bonds can be redeemed.

The Marketing Dictionary

Call System—Arrangement in some selling departments to give each salesperson by numerical rotation, an equal opportunity to wait on customers; commonly used in men's clothing departments, major appliances, and furniture.

Call Tag—Tag or form used by delivery driver to call for, and attached to, an article or package to be picked up at customer's address and returned to store.

Canned Sales Talk—A complete sales presentation which salesmen commit to memory and use verbatim before prospects.

Canvassing—The act of going through a sales territory for such purposes as finding prospects or soliciting sales, subscriptions or advertising.

Capital—An aggregation of economic goods used to promote the production of other goods instead of being valuable solely for purposes of immediate enjoyment or consumption. Produced goods to be used for further production.

Capitalism—The economic system which provides for all or almost all the capital goods to be owned by private citizens, rather than by government.

Capital Funds—Money that is available from individual savers or from groups through savings institutions for investment in business enterprises.

Capital Gain—The profit realized by an investor who buys a security (or capital asset) at one price and later sells it at a higher price.

Capital Goods—The machinery, tools, equipment, etc., used in production. [See Capital]

Capitalization—Total amount of the various securities issued by a corporation. This may include bonds, debentures, preferred and common stock.

Capital Turnover—The ratio between net sales and the average inventory at cost. It is calculated: net sales + average inventory at cost.

Car Cards—Advertising media found on street cars, buses, subways, or on commuter railroad cars, where they may be seen by people on their way to and from work and on shopping trips.

Carrier—A railroad trucking firm, air line, express company, bus line, steamship or river barge company that transports merchandise from vendor to store.

Carrier Transportation—Transporting organization for shipment of goods.

Carrying Charge—A recurring cost incident to the possession or ownership of property, usually regarded as a current expense but occasionally added to the cost of an asset held for ultimate disposition where the market or likely disposal proceeds are judged to be sufficient to absorb the cost thus enhanced.

Carry Outs—Merchandise carried from store by customer, expediting delivery and saving delivery expense, particularly significant in branch stores. Also called "Take-Withs". Must be forward stock immediately available.

Cash Before Delivery (CBD)—"Cash Before Delivery", goods which are paid for before they are delivered to the consumer.

Cash Discount—Percentage off billed price; concession for paying bills within time period indicated on invoice. Cash discounts include anticipation; cash discounts are merchandising gains, included in computing gross margin.

Cash Discount Earned—The discounts for prompt payments of purchases earned on the goods sold during a period.

The Marketing Dictionary

Cash Price—The price charged when payment is effected within a specified interval of time, usually either immediately or within 30 days. It is usually the same as C.O.D. price.

Cash Receipts Report—Form used by salespeople to list cash received from sale of merchandise at end of each day's business.

Cash Register Bank or Fund—Monies given to each salesperson for the purpose of making change.

Cash (for Collect) on Delivery—C.O.D.—An instruction attached to a lot of goods requiring collection of a specified amount of cash from the buyer as the goods are turned over to him or as services are rendered.

Cash Sale—The delivery of goods or the performance of services subject to receipt of cash payment immediately, or, if agreed, within a certain period.

Casual Sale—One that is outside the province of organized business, such as the sale of an old lawn mower by one person to his neighbor.

Caveat Emptor—The principle that the seller (manufacturer and/or retailer) cannot be held responsible for the quality of his product unless guaranteed in a warranty. Literally, let the buyer beware.

Central Buying—Buying activities of a group of centrally controlled or associated stores; generally for merchandise uniformly carried where bulk purchases can influence the purchase price.

Central Control Office—Office charged with responsibility for merchandise control system and accurate accumulation of pertinent statistics.

Centralized Buying—All buying done by merchandise staff located in flagship store or buying center, perhaps located in corporate headquarters or warehouse. Central buying increasingly influenced by requests, suggestions, opinions of branch store managers, and their merchandise staffs.

Centralized management—Where branch offices are not permitted to make major decision s for themselves. The central or home office makes all these decisions.

Chain of Discounts—Granted by the seller to the buyer, the list price is followed by several trade discounts, which are customarily applied in torn to an ever-lessening figure.

Chain Stores—Two or more stores identical merchandise; owned and merchandised by one individual or one company.

Chattel Mortgage Bonds—Securities on which moveable items, such a equipment, is used as security for the bond.

Channel Discounts—A discount comparable to a distributor's discount but differing by being applied against sales to institutional buyers including state and federal agencies and purchasers who further process the product or assemble it in a large unit. Because such purchasers distribute a different product, larger or smaller discounts than distributor discounts may be justified on the ground that a different class of customer is being served.

Channels of Distribution—The routes a product follows as it moves from producer to ultimate consumer.

Character Reference—A statement supplied by employers, acquaintances, schools, and other objective sources, testifying to a person's character and ability.

Charge Account—A credit arrangement whereby a customer is permitted to charge purchases and to pay for them according to some predetermined plan.

Charge-O-Plate—Copyrighted name of small identification plate showing customer has a charge account; plate is used to imprint saleschecks.

Charge-Authorizing Phone—Telephone connecting selling department direct with credit-files section solely for credit authorization calls.

Charter—A corporate charter is usually issued by the state government. It creates the corporation and sets forth its purposes.

Check—A negotiable instrument, payable on demand, which is drawn on a bank for payment of a specified sum of money to a designated person or bearer.

Check, Cashier's—A check which is drawn on the bank that issued it. Used by persons who are dealing with a business firm which may be unwilling to accept a personal check.

Check-Outs—Stations where customers carry self-selected merchandise, pay cashier, and have merchandise wrapped.

Check, Post-Dated—A check dated later than the date on which the check was written. The check cannot be cashed until the date on it.

Check, Stop-Payment—A check which cannot be cashed due to an order written by the payee notifying the bank not to honor the payment.

Check, Traveler's—A special type of check sold through banks by such companies as the American Express Company, used by persons who do not wish to carry large sums of money with them when away from their own banking facilities.

Chislers—Customers who attempt to get store to reduce regular prices for merchandise or services, particularly when buying multiple units, generally more successful with Mama & Papa stores. Also buyers and merchandise managers who try to force prices down from resources.

Chopped Ticket—That part of price ticket removed from sold merchandise and forwarded to vendor rightly as step in vendor's computerized stock control for reorders.

Circulating Capital—Same as Current Assets.

Class Advertising—Is directed at special groups of people, such as newly married couples, golfers, or college students.

Classification—A subdivision of a store or of a selling department for which separate merchandising records are kept but to which expenses are not charged and for which net operating profit is not determined.

Classification Control—System of merchandise control where a classification is controlled by dollar inventory and sales rather than by units.

Classification Merchandising—A type of advertising which appears in columns of a publication under fixed headings, usually in alphabetical order. The yellow pages of a telephone directory are examples of such advertising.

Classified Directory—An alphabetical list of companies and products, contained in a special advertising section of the telephone book.

Clerk Wrap—Name applied to system in which salesperson disposes of entire transaction, including wrappings of "send" merchandise (a semi-clerk wrap is confined to "take-with" transactions).

Close Corporation—When the stock of a corporation is not available for purchase by the general public.

Closed-Door Discount Houses—Sell only to consumers who have purchases memberships. Members are frequently selected from more or less cohesive groups, such as government employees or labor unions, and they are permitted to buy in these stores.

The Marketing Dictionary

Closed-End Issue—When an entire issue of mortgage bonds are sold at one time.

Cluster of Stores—That which will produce enough sales volume in a geographical area to bear cost of advertising, central warehousing, and distribution and provide a profitable operation.

Collateral—Securities or other property pledged to secure the repayment of an obligation.

Collection—The securing of payments from customers who did not pay cash at the time of purchase.

Collection Letter—A business letter or series of letters designed to help in the task of collecting overdue credit accounts.

Collection Procedure—The method established for securing payments of amounts due from credit customers.

Column Inch—One column wide by one inch deep: a print advertising term.

Combination Sale—The sale of a second item or items in conjunction with an established product at an attractive combination price. Usually the second product is a new one which is sold on combination with a well-known product.

Commercial Business—Firms engaged in marketing, such as wholesalers and retailers, firms engaged in finance, such as banks and investment concerns; and in the service field, which includes communication, transportation, gas, electric power, water, supply, hotels, and theaters.

Commercial Goods—Consists of many items that are not intended for use in the fabrication of other goods but which are destined for use in business in the form in which they are purchased.

Commercial Law—The legal rules which relate to mercantile transactions. The body of legal rules governing business intercourse.

Commission—Remuneration of an employee or agent relating to services performed in connection with sales, purchases, collections or other types of business transactions, and usually based upon a percentage of the amounts involved.

Commissionaire—A foreign resident buyer who assists in locating resources and placing orders in a foreign country. The charges a fee which is included in the landed cost.

Commission House—The same as selling agent.

Commission Merchant—An agent who transacts business in his own name usually exercising physical control over goods consigned but not sold to him, and who negotiates the sale of such goods under instructions issued by his principal.

Commitment—A proposed expenditure, evidenced by a contract or purchase order given to an outsider.

Commitments—The amount of merchandise which a store has contracted for delivery during a period. If the period is entirely in the future, the commitments include only outstanding orders. If the period has partly elapsed, the commitments include current outstanding orders plus purchases already received during the durations of the period that has elapsed.

Commodity—Anything which has value and is therefore salable. Everything which is movable that is bought and sold, such as wares, merchandise, and produce.

Commodity Advertising—Designed to sell one or more definite identified commodities, and usually it describes and extols their good qualities or satisfaction-giving features, or their prices.

Common Carrier—Any person who undertakes and is authorized to transport persons or goods as a regular business. Under common law such a person must provide facilities for all that apply at fair and nondiscriminatory rates; and he is held liable for any accident or damage in transit except those attributed to an act of God, a foreign enemy, or carelessness by the person transported or by the shipper of the goods. The liability of a common carrier for any loss or injury to property received by it for transportation is in effect that of an insurer. With respect to passengers, however, the common carrier is liable only for want of proper care.

Common Stock—Securities which represent an ownership interest in a corporation. If the company has also issued preferred stock, both common and preferred have ownership rights, but the preferred normally receives dividends before any are paid on the common stock and, in the event of liquidation, has a prior claim on the corporation's assets. Claims of both common and preferred stockholders come after the claims of bondholders or other creditors of the corporation. Common stockholders assume the greater risk, but generally exercise the greater control and may gain the greater reward in the form of dividends and capital gains. The terms "common stock" and "capital stock" are often used interchangeably when the company has no preferred stock. "Capital stock" also is used to designate all stock both common and preferred. [See Preferred Stock.]

Communicate—To import knowledge of, make known; to communicate information to and from store executives and employees. Adequate communication seriously lacking in many stores, particularly from flagship store or branch store, staff and personnel.

Communication Lack—Failure to notify, inform, or report information, facts, rules or regulations from top management down through the ranks or direct from line personnel.

Communications Mix—Involves the employment of the elements of personnel selling, advertising, and sales promotion in such proportions as to achieve the optimum return to the company.

Community Shopping Center—Usually defined in size as 20 to 40 stores, including one junior department store; on 20 to 25 acres; needing 5,000 family trading area; 100,000 to 200,000 square feet in store area.

Comparison Department—Store department whose function is to compare prices, styles, quality, service, etc., with those of competitors.

Comparison Shopper—Employee in comparison department charged with reporting competitor's activities and merchandise.

Competition—The act of striving for something that is sought by others at the same time. A market situation in which there are many informed and independent buyers and suppliers of the same economic good or service and in which the price is free from government interference.

Competitive Price—The price established in a market by the bargaining of a considerable number of buyers and sellers, each acting independently of the other, no one of them having power enough to dominate the market.

Complementary Skills—Secondary skills that add to and improve the basic skills and abilities important in the performance or duties required for specific responsibilities.

Complement of the Markup—The cost price as a percent of the retail. It may be calculated as 100% minus the markup per cent on retail. Thus, if the markup is 35%, the complement is 65%.

Compliance Bureau—Purpose is to collect, analyze, disseminate, and follow-up the various government regulations affecting the store, particularly in its merchandising and personnel operations.

Complimentary Close—The closing of a business letter after the final paragraph and before the signature of the writer. Such expressions as "Yours truly," and "Sincerely yours," are complimentary closes.

Composition—In commercial law this refers to an agreement by creditors to accept a stated percentage of their claims as a complete discharge in order to avoid long, costly proceedings in bankruptcy.

Comprehensive Coverage—A blanket protection under an insurance contract for practically all risks involving property as combined protection for losses due to fire, theft and casualty.

Consignee—The recipient of merchandise which has beer shipped on consignment. See definition of Consignment.

Consignment Purchases—Vendor's merchandise that is received into a retail stock under an agreement, whereby the store has the right to return to the vendor any portion of the lot unsold within a specified period. Consignment purchases are generally treated as a part of the store's purchase and inventory fixtures.

Consignment Purchase and Dating—Purchase wherein title to merchandise does not pass at time of shipment but at expiration of specified period, when buyer is privileged to return to vendor any unsold goods.

Consignment—Goods shipped for future sale or other purpose, title remaining with the shipper (consignor), for which the receiver (consignee), upon his acceptance, is accountable. Consigned goods are a part of the consignor's inventory until sold. The consignee may be the eventual purchaser, may act as the agent through whom the sale is effected or may otherwise dispose of the goods in accordance with his agreement with the consignor.

Consignor—The owner who ships merchandise to a party on consignment.

Consolidated Delivery—Delivery service of an independent organization which accumulates and delivers packages from various stores.

Consultant—Generally an individual or organization outside of store personnel acting as an advisor. May be a store's retired executive whose experience, ideas, and know-how are valued by top management, working on a part-time basis.

Consumer—A buyer of goods or services.

Consumer Attitude—The viewpoint of consumers on the values or merits of goods and services available to them.

Consumer Cooperation—A retail store owned and directed by its own associated consumer membership.

Consumer Credit—Credit extended by a bank to a borrower for a specific purpose of financing the purchase of a household appliance, alteration or improvement, or piece of equipment which may include an automobile or small aircraft. This credit is generally extended to individuals rather than to businesses. The largest field for this type of financing is in household appliances and home improvements, such as insulation work, furnaces, storm windows and doors, etc. The loan is made for twelve, eighteen and twenty-four months, or longer, and a liquidation agreement is based upon a definite repayment in equal monthly installments. The bank has a chattel mortgage, a lien or a lease agreement as collateral on the commodity purchased and may take possession of the property at any time that the liquidation agreement is not carried out by the borrower.

The Marketing Dictionary

Consumer Demand—The desire for goods and services coupled with the requisite purchasing power.

Consumer Finance—The granting of credit to ultimate consumers by retailers, banks, and other lending agencies.

Consumerism—Interest in the consumer's welfare, how honestly and how well the customer is served, and informed, how accurate and how adequate that information is, how easily it can be understood.

Consumer Motivation—The field of study which explains why consumers act the way they do in buying goods and in patronizing certain businesses.

Consumer Pre-Test—Consists of selecting a group of consumers to whom are submitted samples of advertising copy that have not been released for publication, for the purpose of selecting the one that appeals to them the most.

Consumer Goods—Goods destined for use by the ultimate household consumer and in such form that they can be used by him without further commercial processing.

Comment: Certain articles, for example, typewriters, may be either consumer's goods or industrial goods depending upon whether they are destined for use by the ultimate household consumer or by an industry, or by an industrial business, or institutional user.

Consumer Survey—A form of market research to establish who uses a product, what influences the purchase of specific products. How products are used, and how they are purchased.

Consumption—The use of goods or services for the satisfaction of human desires. Also the use of goods and services for productive purposes, as when raw materials are consumed in the production of the finished product.

Contingent—Regular on-the-payroll member of sales or sales-supporting personnel or employee called in when needed to work part-time or full-time in whatever department assigned to.

Continuous Inventory—A process of testing inventories and of maintaining an equality between inventory item quantities physically determined by count, weight, or measure, and those appearing at the same time on perpetual inventory records.

Contract—A legally binding agreement between two or more parties in which, for a consideration, one or more of the parties agree to do something.

Contract Account—Customer account with stipulated periodic per cent payments.

Contract, Conditional Sales—An installment sales agreement which provides that title remains with the seller until full payment is made. If installments are not paid when due, the holder of the contract may repossess the goods.

Contract Division—Sells to institutions such as schools, hospitals, hotels, motels, and large businesses firms generally at lower markon than retail customers pay. Frequently merchandise is shipped direct from factory to purchaser, bypassing store's receiving, marking, merchandising and delivery departments.

Contract, Illegal—An agreement which is either against the best interests of society or is declared illegal by statute.

Contract Price—The price or price formula stipulated in a contract or purchase or sale.

The Marketing Dictionary

Contract Purchasing—A company enters into contracts with its suppliers covering the purchase of certain materials, the delivery of which will be effected over long periods of time. Reasons-to protect the supply and to take advantage of low prices prevailing at the time the contracts are executed.

Contracts, Tying—Sales agreements which force a buyer to take certain undesirable merchandise in order to secure the particular merchandise he wants.

Control—Any system, device or means of confirming or checking reports, dates, or information (cash register tape is a control).

Controllable Margin—The difference between the gross margin and the direct departmental expenses over which the department manager has a degree of control.

Controlled Shopping Center—Shopping center in which the owners of them frequently determine, in advance of giving leases, the number of stores of each type that will be permitted on the premises. The purpose of this restriction is to afford the tenants a reasonable chance of profitable business by preventing too great a concentration of competing stores.

Control, Sales—A system of supervision involving the use of records, statistics and personal contact for the purpose of exercising control over marketing policies and plans.

Convenience Goods—Those consumers' goods which the customer usually purchases frequently, immediately, and with the minimum of effort. Examples of merchandise customarily bought as convenience goods are: tobacco products, soap, most drug products, newspapers, magazines, chewing gum, small packaged confections, and many grocery products.

Comment—These articles are usually of small unit value and not bulky. The definition, however, is based on the method of purchase employed by the typical consumer. Its essence lies in consumer attitude and habit. The convenience involved maybe in terms of nearness to the buyer's home, easy accessibility to some means of transport, or close proximity to places where people go during the day or evening, for example, downtown to work.

Convertible Bond—Bonds which provide for the exchange of bonds into common stock at the option of the holder during the life of the bond issue.

Conveyance—In commercial law this refers to the transfer of property from one party to another.

Cooperative Advertising—Advertising in payment of which manufacturer, importer, or distributor cooperates with retailer.

Cooperative Display Fund—Definite amount of money provided by vendor, generally matched by store, for development, construction, and installation by store's visual merchandising (display) department to support a specific promotion for vendor's products.

Co-op Money—Co-op: Abbreviation for cooperative, money, what the vendor contributes toward helping promote his goods.

Co-op Wholesaler—Owned and operated by member stores; have no salesmen; selling alone by mail plus two or more "showings" participated by manufacturers two or more times a year at headquarters.

Copy—The text of an advertisement. The main body of writing in an advertisement which is intended to create attention, invite interest, give information and promote action. Any written material prepared for a printer.

Copy Theme—The central idea of an advertisement or of an advertising campaign around which the copy or text is based.

Corporate Bond—A bond issued by a corporation. [See Bond]

Corporation—A type of business organization. An artificial being possessing properties granted it by legal charter, distance from those whose compose it.

Corporation [Closed]—A corporation whose shareowners are all members of a family, or a relatively small group. Its stock is not generally bought and sold by the public.

Corporation [Publicly Owned]—A corporation with many shareowners. Its stock is bought and sold by the public.

Cost—The price at which goods are purchased in the wholesale market.

Cost and Freight (C & F)—The foreign shipper agrees to pay transportation and costs, but not the insurance charges to point stated; title passes when the goods are shipped.

Cost Distribution—The cost or expense which occurs in the marketing of a product.

Costing Sales—Recording the cost price of each item sold on the sales record so that a continuous cost of merchandise sold figure may be available as well as a record of retail sales.

Cost, Marginal—The increase in the total cost of production resulting from the addition of one unit of output.

Cost Method of Inventory—The calculation of the value of an inventory by first determining the original cost price of each item or group of items. Cost codes on price ticket are commonly used for this purpose but serial or reference numbers attached to the goods may allow the determination of cost from other records. The original cost prices may be depreciated if the current market value is deemed to be less than the original cost. Also, the cost of transporting the inventory to the store may be estimated and added to the value of the inventory.

Cost of Goods Purchased—The purchase price of goods bought, plus the cost of storage, and transportation and delivery to the point where they are to be used, and other costs pertaining to their acquisition and receipt.

Cost of Merchandise Sold—The cost to the store of the merchandise that has been sold during the period covered by the operating statement. This figure is also called cost of sales.

Cost or Market Method of Inventory Valuation—Valuing an inventory at the cost price of the items involved or at their current market value, whichever is lower. It is a threefold process, involving (1) taking physical inventory at billed cost prices—determined from cost codes on price tickets or by reference to other cost records; (2) depreciation on items that are not worth what was paid for them; and (3) determining the approximate amount of transportation charges the store has incurred in transporting the inventory to the store—that is considered to be a part of the value of inventory.

Costume Jewelry—Relatively inexpensive jewelry versus jewelry of gold, silver, or platinum, generally set with precious stones. Sometimes related to as "junk jewelry".

Cost Unit—The cost of a single product or service including variable cost and the amount of fixed cost allocated to the product or service.

Cost Variable—The portion of a unit cost which changes, increases or decreases as the output changes, increases, or decreases.

Cost of Goods Sold—The accounting estimate of the purchase price of goods sold by a firm during a particular period. In order to arrive at this figure the company must first determine the inventory on hand at the beginning of the period. To this is added the cost of freight and net purchases. The sum of these three represents the cost of merchandise available for sale. From this is subtracted the inventory on hand at the end of the period. The remainder is cost of goods sold.

Coupon—Many bonds have coupons attached representing the interest payments which are to be made on the bond. The bondholder clips the coupons as they come due and present them for payment of interest.

Coupon Account—Account wherein customer contracts for a certain number of coupons, for which he pays in weekly installments; the coupons can be used as cash throughout the store.

Coupon Bond—Shows no evidence of the owner; the corporation does not know who holds it; and interest is paid to the party who presents the dated coupons which are clipped from the bond.

Coupon Rate—A term often used to mean the interest rate on the bond, for example: $35 interest per year on a $1000 bond is 3.5% interest rate, or coupon rate.

Creative Advertising Director—Responsible for working with merchandise managers, buyers, staff copywriters and art directors in development of fresh, new interesting, informative presentations in various media and in selling information and ideas and for coordination of an idea in the various promotional media.

Creative Packaging—Packaging that creates extra sales by virtue of eye appeal, information labeling, "fresh" appeal; aims to be protective information, revealing easy to house and handle. (Creative packing is sharp, modern, competitive selling tool.)

Creativity—To involve from one's own thoughts or imagination; development of a plan, an idea, a program, a product to fill a need.

Credit—The ability to buy or borrow in consideration of a promise to pay within a period, sometimes loosely specified, following delivery. [See also Consumer credit]

Credit Card—A card which gives its holder the right to purchase goods and services on account. [See Charge-A-Plate]

Credit Crunch—A severe tightening of credit influencing both vendors and retailers due to government efforts to curb spiraling economy.

Credit, Documentary—An account payable in which the credit sale is based on the promise of the buyer as expressed through the medium of a written instrument.

Credit History Card—Record of customer's account indicating home address, employer, account activity, credit limit, delinquencies, past or present, other miscellaneous credit data.

Credit, Intermediate—Credit which is established for a period longer than short-term credit (one year or less) and shorter than long-term credit (ten years or more).

Credit Letter—A written communication usually emanating from the credit and collection department of a company dealing with some aspect of the recipient's credit such as an acknowledgment of a request for credit, refusal of credit or the like.

Creditor—A person group, or company which extends credit; therefore, one to whom a borrower owes money.

Creditor Beneficiary—A third party to whom a promise owes a debt. if the promise contracts with another to pay the debt, the creditor beneficiary can enforce the promise.

The Marketing Dictionary

Creditor, General—A person to whom a debt is owed; who has no claim to preferential treatment in the settlement of bankruptcy proceeding as distinguished from a preferred creditor.

Creditor, Preferred—A person to whom a debt is owed who has a claim to payment prior to the general run of creditors. For example, an employee which wages due has a prior claim over a general creditor.

Credit Rating—An appraisal or classification of an individual's or firm's ability to meet financial obligations.

Credit Transaction—A business transaction in which goods, services, or other values are exchanged for the promise to pay for them in the future.

Credit Union—Cooperatives organized to accept savings from members and to loan these funds to other members.

Cross-Selling—Term applied to sales person's selling in more than one department.

Cumulative Markon %—In dollars, the difference between the delivered cost of merchandise including transportation costs and the cumulative selling prices originally set.

Cumulative Markup %—The initial markup per cent, as calculated from the beginning of the season to a later date or to the end of the season or year.

Current Assets—Includes cash, receivables, and inventories. There is a continuous flow of current assets in the direction of cash as inventories are sold and receivables are collected.

Current Assets—Cash or other assets that will be converted into cash or consumed within a short time.

Current Liabilities—Debts that are owed and payable within a short time.

Customer—A buyer of goods or services, usually on a regular basis.

Customer Complaints—When customers state they are not satisfied with products sold by store—as to size, material content, length of service, color, fastness, cleaning instructions, warranties of guarantees.

Customer Demand—How much merchandise (how many items or how much in dollars at cost or retail prices) customers buy in a stated period of time.

Customer Return and Allowance Percentage—The sum of returns from customers and allowances to customers expressed as a percentage of the gross sales for the period.

Customer's Own Goods-Customer's Own Merchandise—Customer-owned articles, so identified when in for repair, trimming, engraving, etc.

Customer Surveys—Positive efforts to determine what customers in a metro-market prefer.

Cut-Throat Competition—Used when low prices on nationally known or nationally advertised products are used as "bait" to draw customers into a store and efforts are made to switch customer to higher-priced full-profit merchandise (as a rule, assortments of sizes, colors, models, and quantities of bait merchandise are very limited or quantity customer is permitted to purchase is limited.)

Cycle Billing—Correlation of alphabetical breakdowns to specific days of months to facilitating billing of customer's accounts; each breakdown is a cycle and billing for cycle occurs on same day each month.

The Marketing Dictionary

Cycles—As related to business, a cycle is a round or series of economic events that reappear at periodic intervals. The four phases of the business cycle are: prosperity, decline, depression and recovery.

Data—A group of collected facts from which information can be garnered or conclusions drawn about a particular subject.

Dating—A modification of the usual terms of sale, whereby the time of payment is extended owing to circumstances.

Dating Codes—A method of marking price tags with numbers or letters or both in order to keep a record of the age of goods.

Deal—An agreement, such as a purchase order, between buyer and seller, which is fulfilled, will give us to one or more transactions, but which in the unfilled state does not constitute the basis for an entry in the formal looks of account.

Dealer—Typically, a dealer buys for his own account and sells to a customer from his own inventory. The dealer's profit or loss is the difference between the price he pays and the price he receives for the same security. [Contract t his with a broker]

Dealer Aids—Advertising and promotion help given dealers by manufacturers through samples, booklets, displays and the like.

Dealer Financing—A dealer of commodities such as household appliances may make arrangements with a bank for the bank to finance the purchase of these appliances upon their sale by the dealer. The customers who purchase these items then become borrowers of the bank under "consumer credit" or "time sales" loans. The bank usually has the dealer endorse the notes of his customers as additional security for the loans, and has the dealer maintain reserves on each note with the bank as other security. These reserves are termed "Dealer Hold—Backs" or "Dealer Reserves".

Debenture—A kind of bond backed solely by the credit of a company and not secured by a mortgage on the company's property. [See mortgage bond.]

Debt—An obligation of one person to pay money, goods, or service to another person as a result of a previous agreement.

Debtor—A person who owes another person payment for goods or services.

Decentralized Management—Branch offices are permitted to handle their own problem solving.

Decline—A stage of the business cycle often called recession characterized by business apprehension. Production slows down, investors grow wary, industry becomes reluctant to borrow, banks tighten credit, employment sets in, and wages go down.

Deductions from Other Income—Disbursements or losses that pertain to the financing of the business. They include expenses incurred in borrowing and investing funds; losses in the sale of securities and real estate and other financial losses that are not incurred to earn current income.

Default—Any debt obligation which has not been honored according to its terms.

Deferred-Payment Sale—1. An installment sale. 2. Any sale the settlement for which is extended beyond the customary credit period.

Preferred Charge—Also called deferred asset. In accounting, this term refers to an asset, which rises through an adjustment of an expense account, the effort of which is to carry part of the expense forward into the next accounting period.

The Marketing Dictionary

Deferred Liability—Also called deferred credit. In accounting, this term refers to credit which arises through an adjustment of an income account, the effort of which is to carry part of the income into the next accounting period because it has not yet been earned.

Deflation—A fall in prices (caused by a decrease in the supply of money or credit, or both, relative to amount of goods available for purchase).

Delivery—The passage or transfer of possession of goods or services from one person to another, as in a sale.

Delivery, Conditional—Terms or conditions accompanying the delivery of goods, which must be met or accepted before goods will be delivered.

Delivery Expenses—Per cent of sales for cost of delivery, including expenses of packing, wrapping, delivery of merchandise to customer, picking up customer returns, postage, parcel post, and express charges.

Delivery Period—The expected period of time between ordering the merchandise and its receipt into stock. In planning it is receipt into stock. In planning it is prudent to set the delivery period somewhat longer than the normal delivery time to allow for occasional delays.

Delivery, Unconditional—A delivery of goods with no terms or conditions imposed on the receiver.

Deluxe Goods—Higher-priced, exclusive, advance styles or models that wealthiest customers can afford (store may handle deluxe trade without profit for reputation that comes with have this clientele).

Demand—1. The desire by any person for an economic good. 2. The sum total of such desires by all persons, contrasting with supply; in economics, a series of levels each representing a price and the quantity of the commodity or service that buyers are ready to take when the price stands at that level or lower.

Demand, Consumer—The desire by an ultimate consumer possessing the ability and willingness to pay for a good or service offered at any specific price.

Demand, Elastic—A situation which exists when a certain per cent change in the price of a product results in a greater per cent change in demand.

Demonstration Sale—Presented by vendor's representatives-territorial salesmen, demonstrators, or staff trainer, or by member of department's sales personnel, to arm departmental staff with facts, selling points and show better methods of presenting advantages, use, and care of a product.

Demonstrator—Salesperson who devotes all his time to particular manufacturer's products.

Demurrage—Detention of freight car or vessel beyond time allowed for loading or unloading, and subsequent charges for detention.

Departmental Analysis—To analyze department to determine: 1. Whether it is producing its due share of sales volume in that line in store's metromarket, and 2. whether gross margin realized is adequate to cover expenses and contribute to store profits. When unsatisfactory condition is uncovered, detailed studies aimed at improving performance are made, including resources, markon, cash discount, styling, price lining, customer traffic, selling service, advertising, visual merchandising, departmental layout, workroom expense, customer returns and adjustments.

Departmentalizing—Organization of related merchandise and subsequent identification as a department.

The Marketing Dictionary

Department Manager—In both flagship and branch stores department managers are responsible for operation of selling department, freeing buyer to attend vendor meetings, working the market, planning and developing merchandising and advertising programs, devising new floor display ideas, scheduling and training departmental sales personnel.

Department Manager and/or Buyer—Line management, merchandiser; in a one-unit store has both buying and selling responsibilities; in a multi-unit operation is primarily buyer. Analyzes demand, maintains balanced stocks; keeps eye on competition, watches market trends and developments; looks for "hot" new items, manufacturer selling helps, "retail" selling ideas; supervises and deputizes; responsible for profitable operation of department; goes to bat for items, line promotions, money to get what is needed.

Department Operating Statement—Monthly report to department's operation, including sales, stock on hand, markdown, gross margin, expenses, all other pertinent factors.

Department Store—A retail store, or chain of stores, which handles a wide variety of goods, and which is organized into separate departments for promotion, sales, service and control.

Department Store Group—Individual stores that work cooperatively with members of Associated Merchandising Corporation, Allied Store Corporation or May Department Stores, as examples.

Depletion—A term referring to the eventual exhaustion of a source of a natural resource, such as coal, timber, oil or iron. Companies developing or mining, and selling these resources must have plans to provide money to find new sources of supply. The federal government makes tax allowance to companies for this purpose.

Depreciation—A term referring to the wearing out of machines and equipment. Companies must have plans to provide money to replace machines and equipment when they wear out or become obsolete. The federal government makes tax allowances to companies for this purpose.

Depression—A severe, prolonged recession.

Derived Sales—A sales figure obtained from records of purchases and of opening and closing inventory.

Descriptive Billing—Posting of customer's statement in which name of article purchased is written on statement (saleschecks retained by store for adjustment purposes).

Descriptive Labeling—Contents of the can or package are listed on the label.

Design—The intended arrangement of materials to produce a certain result or effect. Industrial design, called structural design, refers to the design of useful products to be mass-produced by machine.

Designer-Picked Fashions—High fashions selected and produced by big name manufacturers.

Design, Package—The design of wrappings, cushioning material, containers and markings to protect items from deterioration to prevent loss and damage, to facilitate handling, to identify and to promote sales.

Detention Time—Charge made by carriers due to lack of facilities and space on store's receiving docks for carrier to unload incoming shipment of merchandise.

Diagnostic Routine—Designed to locate errors in a computer program or malfunctions in the computer itself.

Direct Authorization—Salesperson obtains credit authorization before releasing "send" merchandise to delivery.

Direct Costs—Those that can be directly allocated to the production of a commodity, such as materials and labor.

Direct Expenses—Expenses incurred separately for the benefit of a department within a store. They can be assigned to departments directly and immediately without the intervention of any element of judgement. Direct expenses common to most departmentalized stores are selling payroll, salaries of buyer and assistants, newspaper and shopping news space costs, and delivery charges made by a consolidated delivery service for packages delivered for each department. Normally, these four classes of direct expense total about 40% of the store's total expense. Other expenses may also be directly charged to departments; these include interest on the merchandise investment, supplies consumed, buyers' traveling expenses, and even a rental for space occupied.

Direct Mail—Use of the mails to make announcements, sell merchandise, sell services, sell the store, its divisions, its dependents, its character, and its way of doing business. Personal approach to selective audiences.

Direct Selling—The process whereby the producer sells to the user, ultimate consumer, or retailer without intervening middlemen. The Committee recommends that when this term is used it be so qualified as to indicate clearly the precise meaning intended (direct to retailer, direct to user, direct to ultimate consumer, etc.)

Director of Branch Stores—Usually a vice president, responsible for over-all operation of a store's branches and "goes to bat" for individual store managers with corporation's top management; responsible for volume- and profit-increases in branch stores.

Director of Personnel—Executive responsible for development and activation of store's personnel policies and regulations, in employment, training and performance reviews.

Direct Selling—Vendor selling direct to ultimate consumer, bypassing wholesalers and retailers.

Discharge—The permanent separation by the company of the employee from its service.

Disclaimer Clause—A clause in a contract declaring that the seller excludes any and all warranties in connection with the transaction.

Discount—A deduction from an original price which is allowed for paying promptly or in cash.

Discount, Earned—A deduction from the full price which is realized by paying cash for the goods or service within a stated period.

Discount Merchandising—Low-margin retailing, generally self-service selling goods at less than list price.

Discount, Quantity—A deduction in price given as an inducement to buyers to purchase in larger amounts.

Discounts, Chain—A series of discounts from list price. Chain discounts are generally used by a business firm as ways of announcing price changes without reprinting price lists.

Discount Store—Store operating on lower overall margin than conventional store selling same type of merchandise; generally offers less service.

Discounts to Employees and Customers—Retail reductions taken not because of depreciation but as a matter of policy to give a preferential price to certain favored groups.

Discount Supermarkets—Stores with lower prices base on curtailed advertising, elimination of trading stamps, elaborate inventories, and check-cashing services.

Discount, Trade—A price reduction which is based on the kind of commercial buyer. Also, a price reduction which is used as a device to conceal net cost. This latter is known as a "pure" trade discount, and its practice was banned by the Robinson-Patman Act.

Discount, Unearned—A deduction in price taken after the expiration of a stated discount period, and therefore one which is not due.

Dishonor—The act of refusing to pay a promissory instrument when due or when presented for payment.

Display—Any sign or exhibit, the primary purpose of which is to remind people of the availability of a product or service.

Display Manager—Supervises all window and interior displays, signs, and props.

Display Material—Free display material, including window and counter exhibits, supplied to store by vendor, now considered a form of advertising allowance.

Display, Point of Sale—A display which is located in a retail outlet at or near the place where merchandise is sold.

Display, Window—A display of merchandise in the show window of a business.

Distribution—In marketing, this term refers to moving products from producer to consumer. In statistics, the term refers to the manner in which things being measured are spread between the highest and lowest points on a scale.

Distributive Education Clubs of America—DECA—where high school or other schools prepare students with skills in retailing.

Distributor—A district wholesaler representing one or more manufacturers and having exclusive rights to the distribution of specified products in his territory.

Distress Merchandise—Merchandise which for any reason, must be sold at a sacrifice)at either wholesale or retail level).

Distribution Mix—Choice of channels of distribution which is the most economical and best attuned to the market.

Diversification—Spreading one's investments among the securities of companies in different industries. A company which produces various lines of products is also considered diversified.

Dividend—The payment designed by the board of directors to be distributed among the shares outstanding. On preferred shares, it is generally a fixed amount. Uncommon shares, the size of dividend varies with the fortunes of the company and the amount of cash on hand. Any dividend may be committed if business is poor or the directors decide to withhold earnings to invest in plant and equipment.

Divisional Merchandise Manager—Middle management; executive responsibility for merchandising activities of related group if departments transmits top management policy to line management; supervises department managers (buyer's and manager's assistants; influences decision making supervisory executive.

Dock Areas—Where incoming merchandise is unloaded, generally adjacent to receiving and marking area.

Dollar Control—Control of stock markdowns, markons, markups, and sales in terms of dollars rather than by units of percentage.

Dollar Sales Per Square Foot—Departmental results are derived by dividing each department's net sales by the average number of square feet of selling space occupied by the department. Increasing sales per square feet important objective.

Domestic Corporation—When a corporation is organized under the laws of one state, it is considered to be domestic to that state.

Domestics—Name originally applied to yard goods from which sheets, pillow cases, towels, etc., were cut; now broadly encompasses finished products in these classifications.

Double Decker Stores—Stores in shopping centers with two or more selling floors above street level, generally in enclosed malls.

Draft—An order in writing signed by one party (the drawer) requesting a second party (the drawee) to make payment in lawful money at a determinable future time to a third party (the payee). Drafts may occasionally be written so as to be non-negotiable in that they will not meet all the requirements of the Uniform Negotiable Instruments Act. Drafts generally arise out of a commercial transaction, whereby the seller makes an agreement with a buyer in advance for the transfer of goods. The draft may be made out by the seller (the drawer) ordering the buyer (the drawee) to pay his bank (the payee) for the goods purchased. The draft may be accompanied by a bill or lading or the goods, whereby the bank will surrender the bill of lading to the buyer upon payment of the draft. The buyer can then claim the goods at the office of the carrier who transported the goods to the buyer's place of business. Drafts may be classified as to time element, such as sight or presentation drafts, or demand drafts; arrival drafts; or time drafts. A time draft is presented at sight, accepted and then paid on the agreed-upon date, which may be 30, 60, 90 days or longer after presentation and acceptance.

Drop Ship—When buyer orders merchandise shipped directly to specific branch store, it is noted on order to "drop ship to store." This procedure saves time and expense of vendor's shipping to central warehouse, store's trans-shipping to designated branch; it also means branch store will not be "out" for a long period; sometimes it is more expensive in terms of freight cost.

Drop-Shipper—Also known as desk-jobber. A wholesaler who generally takes title to merchandise but does not warehouse it or stock it since the manufacturer ships direct to the retail customer against orders solicited by and sent in b the drop shipper.

Dual Billing and Posting—Posting customer's purchases to a ledger as separate operation from preparation of customer's bill.

Dual Management Team—Where a chairman of board and president of a store coordinate responsibilities and duties.

Due Date—The date on which a note, draft, or other negotiable instrument is due and payable.

Due Presentment—When a note or bill is made payable on a specific future day, it must be presented to the drawee on that day and payment demand. Presentment one day late results in the holder's losing all rights against the endorser.

Earnings—[See Profit]

Economic Growth—The amount of increase in the value of all goods and services produced by a nation, state, or city. It is usually expressed as a percent increase over the value of the previous year's goods and services. True growth only occurs when the increase is greater than the rise in population and is correct for inflation.

Economic Independence—The ability of an economic unit (family or nation, for instance) to thrive without depending on another economic unit for any goods or services. [See Economic Interdependence]

Economic Interdependence]—The mutual reliance of economic units (e.g., families or nations) on one another for exchange of goods and services. [See Economic Independence]

Economics—The study of the conditions and laws of production, distribution, and consumption.

Economic System—An arrangement of rules under which production, distribution, and consumption of goods and services take place.

Efficiency Index—The return on the average investment in merchandise. The return may be measured at the gross margin level, the controllable margin level, or the operation profit level.

Employee Discount—Discount given employees on purchase of merchandise for their own use.

Enclosed Mall—Shopping center where all store face enclosed central mall with year-round air conditioning.

End-of-Aisle—Spaces fronting on main traffic aisle, particularly important location for 4 1/2-second stopper displays to develop impulse sales.

End-of-Month Dating—Dating which requires the retailer to pay within a certain number of days from the end of the month during which the goods were shipped.

End-of-Month Terms—Indicates time allowance for discount is reckoned from end of month during which goods were bought, not from date of invoice.

Endorsement—When a party writes a legal signature (any signature recognized by law) upon the back of an instrument. An endorsement is required on a negotiable instrument in order to transfer and pass title to another party, who becomes a "holder in due course." An endorsement, in the terms of the Negotiable Instruments Act, has a serious legal significance. The endorser, in signing the endorsement, guarantees that he is the lawful owner of the instrument; that he knows of no informity in the instrument; that he received it in good faith for value received; and that he is a holder in due course, and has the legal capacity to transfer title to another party in the normal course of business. A holder in due course has the legal right to look to any prior endorser of the instrument in case the instrument is dishonored by the maker. Four of the six types of endorsements are: 1. Blank endorsement a general endorsement showing only the signature of the endorser. 2. Special endorsement—the endorser writes the name of the party to whom he is conveying title, as "Pay to the order of John Doe—(signed) Richard Roe." 3. Qualified endorsement—the endorser writes the words "Without Recourse" after the endorsement signature. This type of endorsement is not frequently used, although it does not harm the negotiability of the instrument. The endorser "assigns" the instruments, certifies that he is a holder in due course but restricts his endorsement in that he cannot be called upon for any financial responsibility in case of infirmity in the instrument. 4. Conditional endorsement—an infrequent use of the endorsement in which the endorser places a condition in the endorsement requiring the completion of some act before the endorser can be held financially responsible.

Endorsement, Conditional—The signing of a negotiable Instrument making it payable after a particular event has taken place. For example, the endorsement may be preceded by the statement: "Payable to the order of John Doe when he graduates from a four-year college."

Endorsement, Qualified—A limiting clause append to the signature on a negotiable instrument, freeing the signer from responsibility in the event that the debtor does not honor the instrument.

Endorsement, Restrictive—The signing of a negotiable instrument with some form of restriction over the signature such as the statement "for deposit only."

Endorsement, Special—The signing of a negotiable instrument with the specific person to whom the signer wishes it payable stated above the signature.

End Product—The finished product which goes to the ultimate consumer.

End Sizes—Extreme sizes of an assortment, smallest and largest (which store seldom carries in depth).

Ensembles—Only goods that will harmonize with other goods are bought.

Entrepreneur—Extraordinary person who arranges and manages any enterprise, especially a new or untried business.

Environmental Selling—Displaying merchandise under conditions and settings to these of a customer's own home.

Equipment—Those industrial goods that do not become part of the physical product and which are exhausted only after repeated use, such as Major Installments, or Installation Equipment, and Auxiliary Accessories, or Auxiliary Equipment. Installation Equipment includes such items as boilers,

Linotype machines, power lathers, bank vaults. Auxiliary Equipment includes such items as trucks, typewriters, filing cases, and most small tools.

Equity—The ownership of a company by common and preferred shareowners.

Equity Capital—Funds invested by the owners. This is the major source of long-term financing for sole proprietorships and partnerships.

Esprit de Corps—Loyal employees are working harmoniously along side of, and in cooperating with, each other.

Established Trends—Increased demands for specific merchandise including changes in styles, colors, material content, sizes, price lines as indicated by customer preference or vendor consumer research.

Estimated Physical Inventory—Book inventory minus an estimate of the shortages that probably occurred during the period involved. If the estimate is correct, estimated physical inventory and actual physical inventory will provide the same figures.

European Common Market—The broad purpose of this merger by Belgium, France, Italy, Luxembourg, the Netherlands, West Germany and England is to lay the foundation for the gradual merging of the economics of these nations into a huge common market, to be accomplished by a progressive lowering of their tariffs and trade import quotas.

Even Exchange—Exchange of article of merchandise for one of same price within same department.

Exchange Desk—Station on selling floor servicing exchanges or returns.

Exclusive Agency Selling—That form of selective selling whereby sales of an article or service or band of an article to any one type of buyer are confined o one dealer or distributor in each area, usually on a contractual basis.

Exclusive Merchandise—Confined merchandise not available at other stores in that metromarket.

Executive Trainee—Generally a college graduate who works in various divisions of store while receiving on-the-job training for executive position.

Expenditures—The outlays made during an accounting period. Some are for expense; some for merchandise, and some for the purchase of other assets.

Expense Account—An account set up to reimburse employees of a business for expenses incurred in the execution of certain affairs of the firm. A statement submitted by an employee for reimbursement of expenses incurred in the conduct of affairs of the business.

Expense, Administrative—The same as general expense. [See Expense, General]

Expense Center—A grouping of the expenses having to do with the performance of a specific function.

Expense Classifications—The grouping of expense accounts according to a standard plan.

Expense Distribution—A general term to describe all types of assignment of expenses to selling departments. Some are charged directly to the departments; some are allocated on an appropriate basis and some are prorated.

Expense, Entertainment—The cost of entertainment which is stated in an account and charged to a business as an expense.

Expense, General—Also known as administrative expense. A type of business operating expense which is incurred in the operation of a business apart from the sales effort. For example, the payroll for office personnel other than sales personnel is a general expense.

Expense, Operating—In accounting an operating expense is one which a business firm incurs in the normal operation of its affairs, such as the cost for salaries and wages, for taxes. Operating expenses are divided into selling and general expenses. These are defined elsewhere.

Expense per Transaction—The total operating expenses during a period divided by the number of transactions.

Expense, Selling—A type of business operating expense which is incurred as a result of sales activities.

Expenses—The costs of operating a business other than the costs of merchandise, that are properly chargeable to an accounting period.

Expertise—Expert skill or knowledge; expertness, know-how. A person who has some special skill or knowledge in some particular field; specialist; authority.

Exporter—Dealers which send domestic products abroad for sale.

Express Warranty—A subsidiary promise or a collateral agreement, breach of which does not entitle the buyer to make certain claims for damages against the vendor.

"Extra" Dating Terms—Where these terms apply, the discount can be taken until the expiration of the "extra" period. Thus one finds in the wholesale dry goods trade terms such as 2/10-60 (2 per cent 10 days, 60 days extra). These terms allow the buyer a 2 per cent discount if he pays his bill within 70 days of the invoice date. Another term is 3/10, 2/10-60, which allows a 3 percent discount if payment is made within 10 days, but only 2 percent if payment is made after the tenth day.

Eyeball Control—Use of mark on shelf in warehouse stockroom or forward stockroom to indicate depletion point at which merchandise is reordered.

Fabricated Materials—Those industrial goods which become a part of the finished product and which have undergone processing beyond that required for raw materials but not so much as finished parts.

Factory Cost—Cost of production in a manufacturing establishment.

Fact Tag—Conveys factual information and consumer benefits to salespeople and customers at point of sales; ideally a self-seller.

"Fair Trade" Laws—State laws and the supporting federal Miller-Lydings Act and amendments giving sellers the right to fix minimum resale prices for their products.

Fair Labor Standard Act—Also known as the Wage and Hour Act of 1938. It was the first of a series of federal enactments designed to place a floor under the wages of labor and a ceiling on the number of hours of work per week for workers in private industry whose products enter interstate commerce.

Fair Trade Price—The retail price of a product fixed by the manufacturer under "fair-trade" laws for the purpose of eliminating price competition

Fair Value—The amount that a property will bring, or is worth, in the market as of a specific day.

False Brokerage—Forbids sellers to grant advertising allowances or other services unless these concessions are available to all purchases on "proportionately equal terms." Part of the Robinson-Patman Act of 1936.

Favorable Balance of Trade—The situation where exports exceed imports.

Federal Trade Commission Guidelines—Rules and regulations established by the Federal Trade Commission for vendor in granting advertising and other promotional allowances to retailers whether made direct to retailers or through wholesaler or distributors.

Feedback—Return of information; in retail control systems return of information to vendor (after store's controller has analyzed operation of vendor's line at close of season, buyer and merchandise manager feed back results to vendor, especially in program in which store and vendor have agreed on specific goals).

Field Training—A method of training salesmen under actual selling conditions rather than through a formal sales-training course.

Field Warehousing—A method of storage. It consists of storing of the goods on the premises of he manufacturer or the distributor, with the warehouse company assuming custody.

File, Tickler—A file used to remind a person of things he wants to know on certain dates of the month. A file used to job the memory, such as the filing of vouchers by the dates on which they must be paid.

Financial Ratios—Ratios, such as the ratio between current assets and current liabilities, based on financial information about a business and used for analysis and as a basis for management decisions.

Financial Statement—The statement of a company's financial condition. There are various types of financial statements such as earnings statement and balance sheet. These are usually contained in the company's annual report. They are the source of important information when evaluating the company before investing in its securities.

First-In, First Out Method of Inventory Valuation(FI,FO)—A method of determining the value of an inventory, when costs of individual items in the inventory are not identified, that assumes that goods sell in the order in which received into stock; thus, the goods in the inventory are assumed to be the newest goods purchased and are assigned the cost value code newest goods. Taking inventory at actual cost prices of each item in stock will usually give very similar totals, since goods actually sell in approximate order of their receipt; the retailer makes a real effort to sell the old merchandise first, before the new goods.

Fishyback Freight—Similar to the piggy-back freight of the railroads, in which trucks can be driven onto ships and transported to points nearer their destination.

Fixed Assets—Consists of real estate, machinery and equipment, and other tangible items that have a useful life of from one to many years. Assets that possess a degree of performance extending beyond one year and which are intended for use rather than for sale.

Fixed Capital—Money invested in fixed assets.

Fixed Expenses—Operating expenses in dollars not affected by increases or decreases in sales volume.

Fixed Liabilities—Long-term debts that will not be due for several years.

Fixturing—Layout and selection of fixtures to arrange merchandise for customer convenience; particularly important for self-selection.

Flash Report—Total of daily gross sales by department prepared at close of each business day.

"Flat" Expenses—Variable expenses representing a specific dollar and cents cost for handling a single unit of merchandise or a single sales transaction. Thus, these expenses vary directly with the number of pieces or transactions handled and sold.

Flexibility—Refers to the ability of the advertiser to change his message, if need be, a relatively short time before the advertisement is to appear.

Floating Displays—Moved from location within flagship store or from branch store to branch store.

Flood Light—An artificial light so directed or diffused as to give a comparatively uniform illumination over rather large areas, as in a display window.

Floor Audit (Register Audit)—Accounting for sales transactions in a department or section by using local cash register.

Floor Limit—Arbitrary amount established for floor approval of charge purchases without credit authorization when customer presents proper identification.

Flying Squad—Group or salespeople regular or contingent with exceptional selling ability and flexibility who can be added to any regular department sales staff when needed; also used in sales-supporting and non-selling areas, such as the mail, complaint department, during peak load periods.

Forecast—To form an opinion before-hand; to make a prediction as to sales potentials or acceptance by a store's customers for the acceptance for and purchase of a new product.

Forecasting—The act of making an estimate of future business operations. The immediate or long-range prediction of future sales, production, prices, financial requirements, etc., for the purpose of planning ahead.

Forecasting Sales—The act of making an estimate of dollar or unit sales which will be made during a future period of time under a propose marketing program or plan.

Foreign Corporation—When a corporation is operating in a state other than the one it was incorporated in.

Foreign Exchange—Concerned with the methods whereby buyers and sellers in international trade pay and receive payment for goods and services.

Format—A pre-established arrangement of characters, symbols, lines, areas for presenting or storing data—i.e., the punchcard format.

Forward Buying—Involves orders for larger amounts less frequently. Used when the buyer has room for storage.

Forward Stock—That stock which is carried in the selling department.

Four-Way Audit—Daily sales audit by salesperson, department, kind of sale, and missing saleschecks.

Franchise—1. A privilege, granted by governmental authority, sanctioning a monopoly or permitting the use of public property, usually subject to regulation. 2. The privilege, often exclusive, conferred on a dealer by a manufacturer to sell the manufacturer's products within a specified territory.

Franchise Tax—An annual levy by a state on corporations it has chartered granting permission to continue in business for another year.

Freedom of Contract—Individuals or firms are free to enter into contracts that call for the performance of services or the delivery of goods, provided that there is no violation of law involved, in accordance with the dictates of their own best judgements.

(Free On Board) Destination—**F.O.B.**—Price quoted to retailers includes all transportation costs.

Free On Board Point—Indicates the point at which legal title to the goods passes from seller to buyer. It sometimes indicates the point to which the vendor has agreed to pay transportation charges.

Free On Board Price—The price, when used without further qualification, charged at a designated location, i.e., farm, factory, wellhead, mine mouth, mill or warehouse, where the goods were produced, extracted, fabricated, or stored. Although generally restricted to the price charged at the point of shipment, the term may be qualified by specific reference to intermediate points; e.g. F.O.B. port, or even destination, thus making it the equivalent of delivered price. Under F.O.B. pricing, the seller usually retains title and the risks of ownership until delivery is made at the F.O.B. point, as evidenced by a carrier bill of lading or other receipt releasing him of possession; at that point the purchaser takes title and bears the risk of ownership.

Free On Board Shipping Point—The seller places the goods on a common carrier at the factory loading dock and all further transportation charges are to be paid by the buyer.

Free on Board Pricing—This policy means that the manufacturer quotes prices FOB plant and the buyer pays the freight. This is a system which makes price quotation easy but which causes buyers to have different costs for the goods at delivery points. If the product is sold to industry, differences in freight rates may be important in limiting or expanding markets. If the produce moves through retail channels to consumers, freight rate differences may cause retail price variation between sections of the country. Under this system of selling, a manufacturer has a price advantage near is plant where freight costs are low. Textiles, paper and coal for example are commonly sold on such terms.

The Marketing Dictionary

Freight Inward—Freight paid on incoming shipments treated as an element of cost of goods or materials received, or refunded by the seller or deducted on his invoice, according to the terms of sale.

Freight Outward—Freight paid or allowed by the seller on outgoing shipments to customers. In the accounts it may appear as a selling expense or deduction from sales.

Fringe Assortment—Merchandise for which there is minimum customer demand, therefore slow turnover.

Frozen Account—An account which has been suspended in payment until a court order or legal process again makes it available for withdrawal.

Full Line—Stock of any given classification of goods which includes every variety of style in every color, in every size, and in every material that a customer can reasonably expect to obtain a given price. A full line consists of four definite categories: 1) staples, 2) style merchandise, 3) novelties, 4) outsize (for stock that have a size element).

Full Line Price—A price line at which a relatively complete stock assortment is carried. Three such price lines are often sufficient.

Fully Registered Bonds—Shows the name of the owner on the face of the security; a record of the owner is kept by the issuing corporation; and interest checks are mailed to the holder.

Functional Middlemen—A group designation for a type of wholesaler. The more important wholesalers in this classification are manufacturer's agents, merchandise brokers, commission merchants, selling agents, and auction companies.

Gamble Items—New products that store wants to test for customers' acceptance or reactions.

Gazebo—A display fixture, frequently free-standing, upon which various types of fashion accessories are ensembled.

General Expenses—Costs connected with the general operation of the business; office salaries, rent and taxes are examples of these.

General Merchandise Manager—Top management; participates in major policy making administers policy for entire merchandise division; liaison executive between merchandise division and all other major store divisions; responsible for total store merchandising operation; final work decision-maker.

Geographic Selectivity—The ability of a medium to deliver the advertiser's message to a particular geographic area, such as a designated city or metropolitan community.

Gift Certificate—Certificate suitably engraved, denoting value for which it may be used in lieu of cash throughout the store.

Gift Transaction—Transaction wherein price tickets are removed and instructions for suitable wrapping are included with salescheck.

Gift Items—Merchandise particularly suitable for gift giving; unusual, attractive, appreciated by recipient.

Gimmick—A device or stunt used in advertising or selling to motivate the prospect in the manner desired.

Glossies—Prints of merchandise photographs supplied to store's advertising of display department for reproduction.

Goods—In economics the term means commodities and services. In marketing, it means commodities ad distinguished from services.

Goods in Process—Partly finished product; work in process; raw material and parts on which some labor has been expended in the course of converting or assembling the output of a factory. Under practical operating conditions, the classification may also include raw material and parts removed from stock and waiting the first processing operation.

Goodwill—The price paid for a firm over and above the net fair value of its assets over its liabilities because of the good name, trade connections, or earning capacity of an operating business.

Gourmet—A connoisseur in the delicacies of the table; epicure. Department stores have developed gourmet shops including unusual foods and utensils for food preparation.

Gourmet-Oriented—Merchandise particularly attuned to gourmet preparation and serving.

Governmental Corporation—Organized by the federal government, a state, city, or some other political subdivision. Examples are incorporated cities, state universities, and municipally-owned water companies.

Government Bond—A bond issued by the U.S. Government, including the well-known Series E Bond. [See Bond]

Grace Period—A period after a debt or an insurance premium is due during which a debtor or insured can make payment without incurring a penalty or losing protection.

Grade Labeling—Determination of specific grades of canned goods and the utilization of such symbols as A, B, or C which are placed on the label.

Graphics—Illustration, descriptive techniques including sketches, wash drawings, paintings, water colors, engravings, photographs.

Gross Cost of Merchandise Sold—The cost of merchandise sold before adjustment for alteration costs and cash discounts earned on purchases. It is found by subtracting the closing inventory at cost from the total merchandise handled at cost.

Gross Margin—Difference between net sales and cost of goods sold; the "room to move around in" that determines net operating profit after subtracting operating expense. Shrinkage avoided by careful handling of initial markon, markdowns, discounts.

Gross Margin Percentage—The difference between the net sales and the total merchandise costs divided by the net sales. It may be found from the maintained markup percent by adding the cash discounts earned as a percentage of sales and subtracting the alteration and workroom costs, also as a percentage of sales.

Gross Merchandise Margin—A synonym for gross margin.

Gross National Product—The nation's output of goods and services during the period of a year, expressed in dollar terms.

Gross Profit—Net sales, less cost of goods sold and inventory losses, but before considering selling and general expenses, incidental income, and income deduction.

Gross Purchases (Cost)—The billed cost of merchandise purchased during a period for resale including special charges made by the sellers. Costs of transporting the goods to the store may be regarded either as a part of the gross purchase figure or as an addition to it.

Gross Sales—Total sales, before deducting returns and allowances, but after deducting corrections and trade discounts, sales taxes, excise taxes based on sales, and sometimes cash discounts.

Group Manager—Supervisor in branch store responsible for appearance, the stocks, signing and salespeople selling merchandise that comes from several flagship or main-store departments; usually does no buying, unless reordering staples, keeps "parent" department informed concerning what is selling, what is needed, what is not selling.

Growth Stock—Stock of a corporation which appears to have good prospects for future growth.

Guarantee—A promise or assurance, especially one in writing, that something is of specified quantity, quality, content, benefit, or that it will perm satisfactorily for a given length of time; a money-back guarantee.

Guarantee, Money-Back—A positive pledge that a good or service purchase price will be returned to the buyer if he is not fully satisfied with the good or service.

Guaranteed Price—A price used by sellers to secure sales in an unstable market. To accomplish this objective the seller promises the buyer that in the event of a price decline between the purchase and delivery dates he will reimburse the difference. In some instances this guarantee may extend to the time the goods are finally resold to the ultimate consumer or are used by the industrial buyer. Usually the salesman will require express permission from his company to grant such guarantees.

Guarantor—A person who agrees to fulfill an obligation provided an individual who is responsible for discharging the obligation is unable to do so.

Half Size—Sizing in costs, suits, and dresses for women who are not as tall as the average size.

Half-Tone Reproduction—A technique used in pictures by the use of dots produced by photographing the object behind a fine screen.

Handbills—A form of advertising which is distributed on the street or to the home of the prospective customer.

Hand-to-Mouth-Buying—Practice in which a store orders many small amounts frequently. This may be because of no storage space or limited cash supply.

Hard Goods—Major appliances, including refrigerators, deep freezers, electric and gas ranges, washing machines, dryers, hot water heaters, air conditioners.

Hard Goods Group—Major and minor appliances, home entertainment products, hardware, paint.

Head of Stock—Person responsible for arrangement and identification of reserve and forward stocks.

Hedging—A transaction designed to eliminate or reduce the risk in another transaction. The act of selling against previous purchases of buying against previous sales in order to eliminate as far as possible either loss or gain due to price changes taking place from the time of the original transaction until the time when the materials, goods or commodities are needed.

High End—Most expensive merchandise in a classification.

Hold Slip—Form used to identify merchandise that customer desires to purchase later.

Honor—To pay a note, check, bill of exchange, or other negotiable instrument at maturity according to its conditions.

Honor System—System where in employees record their own working time on time sheets.

Hot Track Record—An outstanding promotion or marketing operation exceeding normal performance.

House Charge—Charge transaction by an employee.

Housekeeping—Presenting merchandise in neat, attractive, orderly manner; keeping stock in good condition in warehouse or forward stockrooms as well as on selling floor; physical maintenance of entire store, also to describe porter and maid service.

The Marketing Dictionary

House Organ—Publication for store's employees. Increasingly important with establishment of more branch stores in disseminating news from top management whom branch store employees seldom or ever see or hear from.

House-to-House Selling—Used to distribute such commodities as cosmetics, brushes, hosiery, and vacuum cleaners.

Housewares Territory—Products that could or should be carried in a complete housewares department but may also be sold in other departments. Housewares has become a major gift department.

Housing—Accommodating stock on selling floor and in stockroom. Every inch of department space is charged on a square foot basis and handling of merchandise is a serious cost factor. (Protective packaging that is compact, self-selling, protective, easy to handle is fine way for manufacturer to win friends and influence retailers).

Huckster—A house-to-house salesman who differs from other house-to-house salesmen in that he carries his stock of goods with him and makes deliveries and he calls repeatedly on the same customers.

Idea Home—Not just a room vignette approach, but showing total contemporary possibilities.

Illegal Reciprocity—An agreement which provides "I buy from you— you buy from me."

Image—Reputation of store; the feelings of customers toward store.

Image Objective—Development of a symbol; a presentation favorable to public opinion.

Impact—In advertising, impact means a forcible impression which a good advertisement makes on the audience at whom it is slanted.

Impact Printer—Data printout device that imprints by momentary pressure of raised type against paper, using ink or ribbon as a color medium, as opposed to photographs, electro-chemical, or other printing means.

Importer—One who deals in goods brought into this country from foreign countries.

Imports—Merchandise manufactured or hand-crafted in a foreign country and imported for sale in a U.S. store. Generally provides a higher than normal markon.

Impulse Buying—The buying of merchandise at the time it is seen without any forethought or preplanning.

Impulse Merchandise—Articles of merchandise purchased on spur of moment by customer without predetermined consideration.

Imputed Interest—Expense for interest charged at a standard rate on the major assets of the business. Imputed interest is generally considerably more than interest actually paid on borrowed funds. The excess of imputed interest over interest paid becomes a credit to other income.

In Bond—Merchandise shipped by manufacturer several months ahead of store's normal selling season is "held in bond" in store's warehouse until selling season; not charged against department's OTB until removed from warehouse to forward stock or selling floor.

Incentive Pay—Bonus or extra commission paid to salespeople for exceeding their production quota.

Incentives—Inducements either financial or non-financial for performance above some standard or designated level.

Income—Money received by an individual company, or other economic unit for performing some economic activity, e.g., wages, rent, sales, interest.

Income, Net—The profit of a business after cost of goods sold and operating expenses, including administrative and selling expenses have been deducted from the net income from sales.

Income, Noncontractual—Earnings such as tips, commissions, or merit bonuses, not based on a fixed standard.

Income, Real—Income received from wages, salaries and other sources in terms of the goods and services which such income will buy.

Income Statement—The statement that summarizes the income and expenses of a business for a stated period of time.

Income Tax—A tax levied on income by government. (If everyone pays the same tax rate, it is a proportional tax; if people with higher incomes pay higher rates, it is a progressive tax.)

Incorporation Fee—This charge varies with the number of shares of stock that the proposed corporation wishes to be permitted to issue, but a minimum fee of from $25 to $100 is customary.

Indenture—Agreement under which the bonds are issued. It spells out the duties of the trustee.

Independent—A business organization, such as a retail store, owned and operated as a private unit as distinguished from a chain of stores.

Index—An average, usually weighted, measuring the change which has taken place in a stated period of time. A series of index numbers shows changes which take place in related items as time passes.

Indirect Costs—Those that cannot be directly allocated, such as occupancy expenses, superintendence, power, and administrative costs.

Indirect Expense—Expenses incurred for the benefit of the store as a whole or for a group of departments. They are often charged to the seller departments on a logical basis but many stores charge direct expenses only against the departments, determining a controllable margin for each. These departmental margins are totaled and indirect expenses deducted to determine the whole store's operating profit.

Industrial Businesses—All businesses that are engaged in producing things by extraction from the earth, by fabrication in the factory, or by construction on a building site.

Industrial Consumers—Are business institutions that purchase goods, usually industrial goods, for use in their business operations.

Industrial Goods—Goods which are destined for use in producing other goods or rendering services, as contrasted with goods destined to be sold to the ultimate consumer. They include land and buildings for business purposes, equipment (installation and accessory), maintenance, repair and operating supplies, raw materials, fabricated materials.

Comment: The distinguishing characteristic of these goods is the purpose for which they are destined to be used in carrying on business or industrial activities rather than for consumption by individual ultimate consumers or resale to them. The category also includes merchandise destined for use in carrying on various types of institutional enterprises. Relatively few goods are exclusively industrial goods. The same article may under one set of circumstances be an industrial good and under other conditions, a consumer's good. In its 1935 Report the Committee sought to pioneer the use of the term business goods as a synonym for industrial goods. Since this suggested usage does not seem to have achieved any significant degree of acceptance, it is now abandoned.

Industry—A field of manufacture in which several companies compete, such as steel, electronics, oil, autos, textiles, etc.

Inflation—A condition of rising prices (caused by increase in the quantity of money or credit, or both, in relation to the amount of goods available for purchase). [See Deflation]

Informative Labeling—Marking merchandise or its packages with specifications of the merchandise and/or with those facts about usefulness and care that will aid customer in making an intelligent choice, and properly using goods.

In-Home Selling—Selling in the home either from "cold canvas" or by appointment made by store earlier. Particularly made by store earlier. particularly applicable for major appliances, furniture, floor coverings, curtains, draperies and decorator upholstery fabrics, sewing machines, vacuum cleaners, television sets, wallpaper, paint.

Initial Markon—Initial and/or first markon used when merchandise is originally offered for sale.

Initial Markup—The difference between the total merchandise handled at retail and the total merchandise handled at cost; expressed as a percent of the retail.

Initial Markup Percentage—The difference between the total merchandise handled at retail and the total merchandise handled at cost divided by the total merchandise handled at retail.

Initial Units—Initial selection of items a line, or classification of merchandise as at beginning of a year or season (any reorders based on customers acceptance).

Installment Account—Credit account in which customer contracts to pay amount by week or month.

Institutional Advertisement—Advertisement to improve image of store or tell customers of a store service, policy or objective.

In-Store Scuttlebutt—Rumors, frequently without foundation, circulated among a store's employees.

Insurance Companies—Organizations that insure individuals and businesses against many types of risks.

Interest—Payments a borrower pays a lender for the use of his money. A corporation pays interest on its bonds to its bondholders. [See Coupon Rate]

Interest Rate—The percent of interest a borrower pays for the use of a lender's money; e.g., $30 interest per year on a $2000 bond is an interest rate of 3%.

Interest Selectivity—The capacity of a medium to deliver the advertiser's message more or less exclusively to groups of customers who would presumably be interested in the product being advertised.

Intermediate Credit—Financing which runs from one to ten years.

Internal Credit—Plan of verification and control for checking store systems for accuracy, validity, and conformity to plan.

Intimate Apparel—Women's, misses, juniors corsets, brassieres, underwear, slips, negligees, robes, lounging apparel.

Intra-store Transfer—Buying goods from one selling department for another selling department within a store.

In Transit—Refers to merchandise that has left consignor's premises and is enroute to its destination.

The Marketing Dictionary

Inventory—The goods on hand at a specified accounting date. The term may apply either to the physical goods or to the value at the time of an accounting.

Inventory Control—The control of merchandise materials, goods in process, finished gods, and supplies on hand by accounting and physical methods. An accounting control is effected by means of a stock or stores ledger or a ledger account in which the quantities or amounts (or both) of goods received during an accounting period are added to corresponding balances at the beginning of the period and amounts of goods sold or otherwise disposed of are deducted at calculated cost based on any various methods of averaging. Physical controls consist of various plans of buying, storing, handling, issuing, supervision, and stocktaking. Stock-ledger control is made more effective by physical control in the nature of a continuous check of the goods on hand.

Inventory Floor Plan—A diagram of the layout of the stock fixtures in a store or department with each fixture and subdivision assigned a distinguishing number. Inventory sheets or tags are assigned to each fixture and a control record is maintained so that, if an inventory sheet or tag is missing, merchandise not yet included in the count can readily be determined.

Inventory, Physical—Determining by actual inspection of the merchandise on hand in store, stockrooms, and warehouses; also recording of this information.

Inventory Recovery—Concept based on a reserve created in expectancy of losses through theft and other causes.

Inventory Sheet—A form for recording the inventory count that provides for the listing of a large number of items on a single form.

Inventory Shrinkage—Takes form of theft, internal or external fraud, record distortion, waste, sabotage, generally laxity, or careless operation.

Inventory Tag—A form for recording the inventory count that provides for the listing of quantity on hand of a single item.

Inventory Turnover—The number of times that the investments in merchandise or stocks on hand is replaced during a stated period, usually twelve months. Merchandise turnover is commonly computed by dividing the cost of sales for the period by the cost of average inventory carried during the period; less correctly, by dividing the amount of sales by the average price. Raw materials and supplies turnover is computed by dividing the cost of the average inventory into the cost of goods issued.

Inventory Valuation—A determination of the proper value of the inventory for profit figuring purposes. The usual rule is cost or market, whichever is lower.

Investment—The use of money for the purpose of making more money, to gain income or increase capital, or both, usually over a long period of time. Safety of principal is an important consideration. [See Speculation]

Investment Banker—Also known as an underwriter. he is the middleman between the corporation issuing new securities and the public. The usual practice is for one or more investment bankers to buy outright from a corporation a new issue of stocks or bonds. The group forms a syndicate to sell the securities to individuals and institutions. Thereafter, the market in the security may be over-the-counter, on a regional stock exchange, the American Exchange or the New York Stock Exchange. [See over-the-counter, syndicate]

Investor—An individual, group or institution which owns stocks or bonds, or other forms of equity, such as real estate.

The Marketing Dictionary

Invoice—A bill prepared by a seller of goods or services and rendered to the buyer. The invoice usually itemizes all items marking up the bill for the convenience of the buyer, and to prevent disagreements regarding the amount of the bill. Invoices are used as posting media by the seller in his accounts payable. Invoices are also used in preparing shipments by the seller, and in receiving goods by the buyer.

Invoice Cut-off—Setting a specific time after which invoices received will not be included in the calculation of the inventory on hand. After this time, the merchandise corresponding to these invoices will not be included in the physical inventory count.

I.O.U.—An abbreviation of "I owe you." An admission that a debt is owed, but not a promise to pay.

Item—A specific style, color, size, or price of merchandise.

Item History—Record of movement (sale of a specific item, line, or assortment of merchandise.).

Job Analysis—All the pertinent facts relative to each job. Involves inquiry into all the details of each position in the company that the personnel department might be called upon to fill.

Jobber—This term is now widely used as a synonym of wholesaler.

Comment: Formerly the jobber was a dealer in odd lots but this usage has practically disappeared. The term is sometimes used in certain trades and localities to designate special types of wholesalers. This usage is especially common in the distribution of agricultural products. The characteristics of the wholesalers so designated vary from trade to trade and from locality to locality. Most of the schedules submitted to the Bureau of the Census by the members of the wholesale trades show no clear line of demarcation between those who call themselves jobbers and those who prefer to be known as wholesalers.

Therefore, it does not seem wise to attempt to set up any general basis of distinction between the terms in those few trades or markets in which one exists. There are scattered examples of special distinctive usage of the term jobber. The precise nature of such usage must be sought in each trade or area in which it is employed.

Job Description—The information that is gathered during the job analysis which relates strictly to the job itself and in writing.

Job Lot—Miscellaneous group of assortment of style, sizes, colors, etc., purchased by store as a "lot" at a reduced price.

Job Order—An order authorizing the production of a definite number of units of product, the construction, or repair of specified equipment, or the rendition of specified services; known also as a production, construction, repair, or service order, it may serve as the basis for the accounts or subaccounts in which costs are recorded, grouped, and accumulated.

Job Specification—A statement of the personal qualifications required of prospective employees for each type of job, such as skill, age, experience, and special aptitudes.

Knockoff—Close reproduction of design of a textile or apparel product. Differences in the copy may be shadings in color (not easily apparent to public), smaller size, less weight; often refers to foreign "knockoffs", which sell for lower prices than American original.

Labor Turnover—Voluntary resignation of (experienced) employees, replacing the with inexperienced workers, possibly, in lower salary classification.

Last In, First Out Method of Inventory Valuation (LIFO)—A method of determining the value of an inventory by assuming 1) that it is necessary to carry a fixed basic inventory assortment that has a fixed valuation and 2) that the sales made represent the newest goods purchased at prevailing prices. Thus, the so-called basic stock does not fluctuate with changes in the price level. During inflation, inventory is valued at a lower figure than under FIFO or when a determination of the actual cost prices of the goods in the inventory may be made.

Lay-away—Method of deferred payments in which merchandise is held by store for the customer until completely paid for.

Leader—A selected item that is deliberately sold at a price lower than the one at which the largest total profit on the item could be realized in order to attract customers.

Leased Department—Department operated by outside organization, generally on percentage-of-sales basis. A lessor must abide by rules, regulations, operations, and objectives of lessee.

Ledger Card—Record of customer's charge account activity and bill payments, kept in accounts receivable files.

Less-than-Carload-Lot—A term referring to shipment of which requires less space than available in a single freight car, or to the freight rate applicable to such a shipment.

Leverage—The influence of changes in sales volume on profits caused by fixed expenses. A relatively small increase in sales normally causes a relatively large increase in profits since many expenses are fixed. Conversely, a small sales decrease normally causes a large decrease in profit.

Liabilities—All the claims against a corporation, that is, all the money it owes or is required to pay out, such as wages and salaries, declared dividends, accrued taxes, bonds, and bank loans. [See Assets]

Lien—The right of one person to satisfy a claim against another by holding the other's property as security or by seizing and converting the property under procedures provided by law.

Limited Liability—The shareholder in a corporation risks only the amount he invests in the corporation. If the company proves unprofitable and fails, creditors cannot look beyond the assets of the corporation for funds to settle their claims.

Limit Order—A customer's order to a securities broker to buy or sell at a specific price or better. The order can be executed only at that price or a better one.

Linage—Measurement of number of lines to a column or full page of advertising in a newspaper or magazine advertisement.

Line—An agate line; a vertical measurement of a column of type; 14 lines to an inch.

Line of Credit—An agreement between a bank and a customer whereby the bank agrees to lend the customer funds to a previously agreed maximum amount. The bank has the option to withdraw from the agreement if the financial status of the borrower changes, or if the borrower fails to use the line of credit for its intended use as per the agreement. The customer may borrow as much of the "line" as is required and pays interest on the borrowed portion only. A line of credit is widely used by large organizations for the future commitments and purchases of inventory. The bank is fully entitled to periodic financial reports from the borrower so as to be constantly informed on his credit status.

Line Organization—Is one in which there is a direct flow of authority from the top executive to the rank-and-file employee, usually through several lesser executives at various managerial levels.

The Marketing Dictionary

Liquidation—The process of converting securities or other property into cash. Also, the dissolution of a company.

Liquidity—The ability of the market in a particular stock to absorb a reasonable amount of buying or selling at reasonable price changes. Liquidity is one of the most important characteristics of a good stock market.

Listed Securities—Stocks and bonds that have been approved for trading by security exchanges.

Listed Stock—Usually, the stock of a company which is traded on a securities exchange.

List Price—A printed [published] price, as one appearing in a catalog, subject to trade and cash discounts.

Loading—The amount added to an installment contract to cover selling and administrative expenses, interest, risk, and sometimes other factors.

Loading of Cash Discount—Building up gross invoice price of merchandise and crediting cash discounts with the amount of the load. It may be done by the resource through an adjustment of the invoice or, more often, by the store's, through a bookkeeping entry.

Lobby Window—Generally a small display window directly inside a door leading into store from street.

Locker Stocks—A shipment by a manufacturer or wholesaler of extra inventory assortment, which is held in store's central warehouse unopened (not consignment selling); as soon as buyer needs any item being held in locker stock, payment becomes due to vendor for entire shipment.

Logistics Mix—Concerned with the physical distribution of goods; it involves the selection of storage and transportation facilities in such a combination that the merchandise is moved from producer to purchaser at the lowest cost consistent with the purchaser's demand for service.

Long Pull—Planning future growth for a store, a department, a classification, or a service based on a study and analysis of potential factors.

Long-Term Contract—Any contract for goods or services the completion of which extends into one or more succeeding fiscal years. The term is often applied to agreements covering the production of heavy equipment such as electric generators, construction projects, and ships. The propriety of the accrual of revenue by the producer, as sections of the work are completed, has long been recognized in accounting.

Long-Term Financing—Funds from owners and loans that mature in several years, usually ten or more.

Loss Leader—A selected item that is deliberately sold at less than cost in order to attract customers.

Low End—Least expensive merchandise in a classification.

Low-Margin Retailing—Discount or mass merchandising.

Made-to-Measure—Men's suits and overcoats, draperies, slip covers, and floor coverings are cut and sewn to fit. Generally results in larger sales book.

Mail-Order House—Sell and deliver goods by mail, making use of catalogs, newspaper advertising, and direct mail to attractive customers.

Maintained Markon—Difference between net sales and gross cost of sold goods.

Maintained Markup—The difference between the net sales and the gross cost of merchandise sold. It is the margin on sales before making adjustments for cash discounts earned and alteration costs.

Maintained Markup Percentage—The difference between the net sales and the gross cost of merchandise sold divided by the net sales.

Maintenance Supervisor—Responsible for upkeep and operation of electrical equipment and lighting, year-round air-conditioning, vertical transportation system, telephone system.

Management—The individuals charged with the responsibility of operating business enterprises and of endeavoring to do so profitably.

Management by Objectives—Program of professional management techniques and merchandise as well as economic trend indicators to keep ahead of competition, strengthening management at store and corporate levels. These are geared to the goal of increasing sales per square foot—one of the key factors that measures earnings in retail business.

Managing An Inventory—Meeting monthly peaks and valleys, in any line of merchandise, by increasing inventory prior to peak selling periods, reducing it at peak wanes.

Manhours—The summation of all the productive hours worked by all employees in a work center during a period. It includes the scheduled hours worked by supervisors.

Manifest—Shipping form used by carriers for consolidation purposes, listing all pertinent information used by carriers internally to list contents of a particular vehicle, listing same information used by carriers internally to list contents of a particular vehicle, listing same information; also used by stores in transfer operations from central warehouse to branches.

Man-made Fibers—Fibers produced by chemical or mechanical processes versus natural fibers from animals, insects, or plants.

Mannequin—A clothes model; a styled and three-dimensional representation of the human form used in display windows and on ready-to-wear selling floors to display apparel.

Manufacturer's Agent—An agent who generally operates on an extended contractual basis; sells within an exclusive territory; handles non-competing but related lines of goods, and possess limited authority with regard to prices and terms of sale. He may be authorized to sell a definite portion of his principal's output.

Manufacturer's Representative—Selling agent, preferably retail-minded, capable of giving informative talks to selling personnel.

Margin—1. Gross profit. 2. The excess of the market price of collateral over the loan it secures.

The amount paid by the customer when he uses credit to buy a security, the balance being lent to him by the broker. The Federal Reserve Board regulates the amount of credit which may be supplied by brokers and banks in the purchase of most securities by their customers.

Markdown—Reduction in retail price of merchandise, primarily for clearance of broken assortments, end sizes, prior stock, for special sales events, and to meet competition.

Markdown Cancellation—An increase in price caused by marking goods back to the original retail price.

Markdown Goods Percentage—The dollar sales of goods marked down divided by total sales. Assuming carryovers of markdown goods in opening and closing inventories are the same, the mark-down goods percentage may be found by subtracting the dollar markdowns from the original retail prices of markdown goods and dividing by the total dollar sales.

Markdown Percentage—The net markdowns taken during a period divided by the net sales.

Markdowns Off Percentage—The dollar markdowns divided by the original retail price of the goods marked down. This relationship is the one that the general public regards as the markdown percentage. If all the merchandise handled is sold, the original retail price is the same as the sales plus the markdowns. When opening and closing inventories are involved, the original price of the goods marked down approximates the sales plus the markdowns for the period, on the assumption that markdowns reflected in the opening inventory are probably balanced by markdowns in the closing inventory.

Markdown Timing—Selecting the time to take markdowns relative to the length of the selling season still remaining.

Market—Where retailers buy merchandise; a place, the people!

Marketability—The ability to readily sell a security at a reasonable price.

Market Demography—Science of vital statistics of population (households, marriages, births, age groups, marriages, births, age groups, incomes, sales by peak hours of the day, days of the wee, and months of the year)>

Marketing—The performance of business activities that direct the flow of goods and services from producer to consumer or user.

Marketing Cost—The cost of locating customers, persuading them to buy, delivering the goods, and collecting sales proceeds; selling cost.

Marketing Functions—Inescapable tasks that must be performed in the marketing of products. Buying, selling, transportation, storage, standardization, market finance, risk bearing, and market research are commonly grouped together as the marketing functions.

Marketing Institutions—Another term for marketing middlemen.

Marketing Research—The gathering, recording, and analyzing of all facts about problems relating to the transfer and sale of goods and services from producer to consumer. Among other things it involves the study of the relationships and adjustments between production and consumption, preparation of commodities for sale, their physical distribution, wholesale and retail merchandising, and financial problems concerned. Such research may be undertaken by impartial agencies or by specific concerns or their agents for the solution of their marketing problems.

Market Minimum—A price set below the customary market price in order to attract customers. It may be temporary to eliminate competition or it may be permanent, made possible by lower-than-average expenses per transaction.

Market Penetrations—A store's share of a metromarket in a specific department or classification of merchandise within reason there is no limit on how deep a penetration successfully-operated departments can make.

Market Potential—The expected sales of a commodity, a group of commodities, or a service for an entire industry in a market during a stated period.

Market Price or Value—Recent invoice or quoted price at the close of an accounting period, less customary adjustments, including cash discounts; the price at which a seller willing to sell at a fair price and a buyer willing to buy at a fair price will trade, assuming that both have a reasonable knowledge of the facts, that similar quantities, qualities, and delivery periods are involved, and that the market has been canvassed by both buyers and sellers.

The Marketing Dictionary

Market Order—An order by a customer to a broker to buy or sell at the best available price when the order reaches the trading floor.

Market Price—The last reported price at which a stock or bond was sold. This price can change from minute to minute, depending on market conditions.

Market Representative—Member of resident-buying-office staff whose major responsibilities are to act as market shopper, analyst, merchandise counselor to merchandise manager and buyers of office's member store; also expedites shipment of initial orders and reorders placed by member stores.

Marking—Putting the correct price tag on new merchandise.

Markon—Difference between cost price as billed (before deductions for cash discount) and retail price at which merchandise is originally offered.

Markup—The difference between the cost and the retail price of merchandise. In equation form: Markup - Retail - Cost.

Markup Percent on Cost—The markup divided by the cost. Markup percent on cost is higher than markup percent on retail. The generally accepted plan is to express markup on retail, even though markup percent on cost is the older method.

Markup Percent on Retail—The markup divided by the retail. The term, percent of retail, means the same as percent on retail.

Masking Piece—A flat curtain blocking part of a store window; concentrates shopper's attention or hides work in progress.

Mass Advertising—Advertising that appeals to a cross-section of the populace.

Mass Merchandising—Self-service store displaying and selling all kinds of merchandise; displays tend to be massive; customers usually push wire carts to collect and carry their own selection of merchandise to cashier checkout counters.

Mass Production—A manufacturing technique that end only results in the creation of a great quantity of goods but also brings about a reduction in unit costs, which, in turn, permits lower prices and greater sales.

Material Control—The supplying of commodities required in manufacturing at the lowest cost per unit consistent which required quality and with the least investment in inventory.

Maturity—The date on which a bond or debenture comes due and is to be paid.

Maximum—The amount of stock that should be on hand and on order just after a reorder is placed.

Media—1) Evidence of transactions with customers (saleschecks, vouchers, return slips, etc.). 2) As used in advertising: periodical (newspaper, magazine, shopper publications); direct (direct mail, catalog); sign (outdoor or indoor poster, bulletin, sign, point-of-purchase, car-card transit sign); sky-writing; motion pictures; program (theater, menus, guides); broadcast (radio, television, public address, loud-speaker systems).

Media Mix—Planning use and coordination of advertising and promotional media, such as interior and exterior display, and newspaper, direct mail, radio, T.V., magazine, transit, and outdoor advertising.

Media Representatives—Sales and/or service representatives from newspapers, radio, T.V., and direct mail media who service store accounts.

Member Corporation—A brokerage firm, organized as a corporation, with at least one director, a holder of voting stock, who is a member of the New York Stock Exchange.

The Marketing Dictionary

Member Firm—A brokerage firm, organized as a partnership and having at least one general partner who is a member of the New York Stock Exchange. In general usage, member firm includes the term, member corporation.

Memorandum and Consignment Selling—Vendor agrees to take back goods if they are not sold in a specific period of time. Since the markdown risk is borne by the vendor, the buyer's maintenance is equal to his initial markon. Under the memorandum arrangement, title passer to the buyer, ordinarily, when goods are shipped, but vendor assumes contracted obligation of taking back unsold portion of goods at a specific time. On consignment purchase, title does not pass to store but instead passes directly from vendor to store's customers—store acts simply as an agent for vendor. Vendor can control retail price.

Merchandise—Agent middlemen whose task it is to negotiate transactions between sellers and buyers without having direct physical control of the goods.

Merchandise Charge—Extraneous costs, such as shipping charges, insurance, demurrage, etc., applicable to cost of merchandise prior to markon.

Merchandise Classification—Applied to a merchandise group within a department and controlled by dollar volume rather than by units.

Merchandise Control—Department that maintains accurate figures on purchases and sales merchandise, either by dollar or by units.

Merchandise Controller—Takes off buyer's shoulders problem of distribution of merchandise to departments and of reordering.

Merchandise Manager—Often synonymous with title of divisional merchandise manager. Sometimes a separate executive responsibility, under divisional merchandise manager, for merchandising activities of one or more selling departments.

Merchandise Manager Counter-Signing—Signature of merchandise manager in addition to buyer's signature on purchase orders required by many stores. This confirmation gives merchandise manager control over order.

Merchandise Management Account—New concept of accounting by which net profit contribution of merchandise is figured before goods are purchased.

Merchandise Marts—Building housing showrooms for manufacturers and importers where, under one room, store buyers and merchandise managers can inspect lines from resources in minimum time. The Merchandise Mart in Chicago is reported to be the largest in the world.

Merchandise Plan—A forecast, usually by months for a six-month season, of the major elements that enter into gross margin. It normally includes sales, stocks, purchases, markups and markdowns.

Merchandise Shopping—May be initiated 1) by buyer or merchandise manager; 2) by the customer; 3) by the want-slip system; 4) by the advertising manager before preparation of an advertisement.

Merchandise (or stock) Shortage—The discrepancy between the amount of merchandise that the store's records indicate should be on hand and the amount actually on hand. It reflects 1) physical loss and 2) errors in record keeping in counting. Shortages may be calculated at cost value, retail value, or in units, but when they are included in retail reductions, they are always calculated at retail. Synonymous with stock shrinkage.

Merchandise Specification—Buyer sets up or obtains specifications for qualities expressed in necessary technical terms. Proper specifications cannot always be determined until needs and expectations of customers have been carefully analyzed and until some experimental work has been done.

Development of private brands or controlled brands has increased need for rigid specifications prepared for or by the store's merchandise divisions.

Merchandising Division—The division of the store that is responsible for planning stock assortments, for buying and for merchandising control. It is often held responsible for sales results, too, even though it may not supervise the selling and publicity staffs. Along with the controller and top management, it shares in the responsibility for balancing the growth and profit factors.

Merchandising Operating Results—The annual report, Department of Merchandising and Operating Results in Department and Speciality Stores, published by the controllers congress of the National Retail Merchants Association.

Merchandising Technique—Technical skill, ability to apply procedures or methods so as to attain specific goals in manufacturing and/or retailing.

Merchant—Anyone engaged in buying and selling at retail.

Merchant Wholesaler—Wholesale establishments that buy and sell on their own account; that is, they take title to the goods which they handle.

Metromarket.—Center city plus suburban areas from which a retail store draws major portion of customers.

Middle Management—Secondary layer of divisional managers, i.e., assistants.

Minimum—Amount of stock planned to be on hand at the moment a reorder is placed. It is sufficient to cover probable sales during the delivery period and to provide for a safety factor.

Minimum Stock Control—Method of reordering staple merchandise on basis of predetermined minimum quantity; when minimum is reached, quantity of initial order is again purchased.

Model Stock—A planned assortment of units of merchandise balanced to anticipate customer demand and resulting in the planned stock-turn.

Mom and Pop Outlets—Small stores generally operated by husband and wife with limited capital, in a restricted selling area composed of low income families. Very dependent on wholesaler and/or distributor for financial support.

Money Capital—Money which is saved—not spent on consumer goods; money used by business to purchase machines, equipment, buildings, materials for production.

Monopolistic Competition—There are many makers of goods with identical end usage who brand their products to differentiate them from those of their competitors.

Monthly Investment Plan (MIP)—A pay-as-you-go method of buying a New York Stock Exchange listed shares on a regular payment plan for as little as $40 a month, or $40 every three months. Under MIP the investor buys stock by the dollar's worth. If the price goes up, he gets fewer shares, and if it declines, he gets more shares. He may discontinue purchases at any time without penalty. The only charge for purchases and sales is the usual commission for buying and selling, plus the regular odd-lot dealer differential. The commission ranges from 6 per cent on small transactions to slightly below 1 1/2 percent on larger transactions.

Mortgage Bond—A bond secured by a mortgage on real property.

Most Profitable (MP)—An item carried in a price line that is most profitable from the standpoint of the merchant.

Multinational Business—Firms whose home bases are in the United States, but whose operations extend to many parts of the free world.

Multiple Price—A price placed on a number of identical or similar articles or on a set of related articles that is less than the sum of the unit prices of the articles. For example: tennis balls - 3 for $1.17 or 45¢ each.

Multiple Sales—Encouraging customers to buy multiple rather than single items.

Municipal Bond—A bond issued by a state or a political subdivision, such as county, city, town or village. The term also refers to bonds issued by state and local agencies and authorities. In general, interest paid on municipal bonds is exempt from federal income taxes. [See Bond]

Mutual Funds—Same as investment companies.

Name Advertising—Type occurs when the nature of the product, its ingredients, the manner in which it is used, the product benefits to be expected, or the fact that it is very well known to the public suggests the desirability of advertising its name, with non-technical copy, often in an attractive setting. Name advertising is commonly used for soft drinks, aspirin and cosmetics.

National Brand—A manufacturer's or producer's brand usually enjoying wide territorial distribution.

National Retail Merchants Association—The only national retail trade group specifically functioning in the interests of nation's department chain and speciality stores; and non-profit voluntary membership organization with administrative headquarters in its own N.Y.C. office building and branch offices in Washington, D.C., San Francisco and Paris.

Natural Business Year—A fiscal year ending with the annual low point of business activity or at the conclusion of a season.

Negative Authorization—System of credit authorization in which a list of delinquent accounts is maintained (if customer's name does not appear on this list, her request for credit is approved).

Neighborhood Shopping Center—Or "strip center": 10 to 15 stores, including food, drug, sundry, and personal service stores; 5 to 10 acres; needs at least 1,000 families trading area for support, usually under 100,000 square feet.

Net Alteration Costs—The difference between the cost the store incurs in performing the alterations and the amounts, if any, paid by the customers for this service. It is treated as an addition to the gross cost of merchandise sold.

New Book Value—The difference between the gross amount of an asset or asset group as shown in the books of accounts and any reserve or other applicable offset such as accrued depreciation.

Net Cost of Merchandise Sold—The gross cost of merchandise sold less than cash discounts earned. It is the same as net cost of sales.

Net Other Income—The difference between other income and deductions from other income.

Net Period—The time allowed to pay a bill without deduction of a discount.

Net Profit—The sum of operating profit and net other income. Also called net gain.

Net Profit on Sales—The balance remaining after deducting from gross profit on sales selling and other expense varying directly with sales; also known as net trading profit.

Net Purchases—The cost of purchases plus freight-in [See "freight inward" above], less returns and allowances and often cash discounts taken.

The Marketing Dictionary

Net Sales—Gross sales less returns and allowances, freight-out, and often cash discounts, allowed. In recent years the trend has been to report as net sales the net amount finally received from the customer.

Net Terms—A condition of sale calling for the payment of the billed amount of the invoice at a specified date with no cash discount reduction.

Net Worth—The owner's equity in the store. The difference between the assets and liabilities. Profits are commonly expressed both as a percentage of net worth and as a percentage of net sales.

Noncumulative Preferred Stock—No dividends omitted in previous periods need not be declared before any action can be taken leading to a distribution of profits to the common shareholders.

Nonparticipating Preferred Stock—Limits the annual dividends to the amount stated at the time of issue.

Nonprice Competition—Competition between rival sellers who charge identical or comparable prices but appeal to consumers by claiming superiority in such items as quality, service, style, packaging, reputation and prestige. In recent years, competition of this character between business concerns has been growing, and business standards are often evolved to discourage unilateral price action by an individual seller. Price changes now tend to be made on the basis of industry-wide action in recognition of modified economic conditions such as increased wage rates or raw-material costs, the impact of new demand created by government procurement, and other "market conditions" not always specified. In industries where price competition does exist, the same practices identified on nonprice competition may also be present.

Non Profit Corporation—Receipts may exceed its disbursements by a distribution is never made to its owners, and any income that may result from its operations is used to further the purposes for which it was organized.

Non-Salable—Merchandise soiled or damaged beyond reclamation or sale-ability; generally disposed of to charitable organizations.

No-Par Stock—Preferred stock with no stated value printed on the face of the certificate.

Number of Stock Turns—Stock turnover is calculated by dividing average inventory at retail into the net sales for the year. Average inventory is the sum of the retail inventories at the end of each month added to the initial opening inventory and divided by thirteen, the number of inventories used.

Odd-lot—An amount of stock less than the established 100-share unit or 10-share unit of trading; from 1 to 99 shares for the great majority of issues, 1 to 9 for so-called inactive stocks. [See round lot].

Offer—The price at which a person is ready to sell, as opposed to bid, the price at which one is ready to buy.

Oligopoly and Oligopsony Prices—An oligopoly price is the price that prevails in a market of few sellers and many buyers: a price reflecting the power of a few large sellers may exert over the market. An oligopsony price is the price that prevails in a market where buyers are few and sellers numerous: a price reflecting the power a few large buyers may exert over the market. Oligopoly prices tend to be greater (and oligopsony prices less) than prices that would prevail in perfectly competitive markets. Where a few sellers (oligopoly) confront a few buyers (oligopsony), price is determined by relative bargaining power.

One Price Policy—A policy to sell to all customers at the same price. This does not preclude 1) the taking of markdowns so long as the reduced prices are available to all customers; 2) the offering of multiple prices; and 3) the granting of discounts to employees.

The Marketing Dictionary

One-Shot Promotions—Merchandise manufactured for specific event; imports that cannot be reordered.

One-Stop Shopping—Everything a customer would need for self, family, home; located under one roof.

On Account—1) On credit terms; said of a sale or purchase in which delivery is followed by payment at a later date; 2) in part payment: a term applied to the settlement of a portion of a debt.

On Consignment—Consigned to another for the purpose of sale, display, or other use.

On Hand—In possession, whether or not owned.

On Order—Applied to merchandise purchased but not yet received.

Open Account—Credit extended to an individual, firm, corporation or other legal entity based on an estimate of the general ability to pay, as distinguished from credit extended that is supported by a note, mortgage, or other formal written evidence of indebtedness.

Open Corporation—When the stock of a corporation is available for purchase by anyone having the money necessary.

Open Credit—An unsecured receivable or payable not evidenced by a note, subject to settlement in accordance with usual trade or other specified terms.

Open-End Issue—Permits the sale of additional bonds at a later date under the original mortgage.

Open Order—Order placed without price or delivery stipulation; order sent to market representative in resident buying office without specifying vendor.

Open Stock—Additional and/or replacement pieces of merchandise (example: dinnerware) carried in bulk and kept in stock for several years. Open stock slows turnover materially.

Open to Buy—A term used in retailing, particularly department stores, to designate a stated amount of money or merchandise to which a buyer is limited in his purchases.

Open to Buy by Classifications—OTB for a specific line, number, or item through department as whole is over-bought (or, more factually, undersold).

Open-to-Spend—The difference between an expense budget for a period and the amount spent to date, when the former is the larger.

Operating Expenses—The costs a business incurs in its normal operations, such as wages, purchase of materials, power costs, maintenance of equipment, etc.

Operating Management—Plant supervisors and foremen and the heads of subdivisions of the larger departments.

Operating Profit—The business gain realized from trading operations alone. It is the difference between sales income on the one hand and the cost of merchandise sold plus the operating expenses on the other.

Operating Statement—An analytical presentation in figures of the income, costs, and expenses of a business for an accounting period, such as a month, a season, or a year.

Order Follow-up—To insure vendor shipment on time, stores develop an organized follow-up system, orders arranged by due date; on due date vendors are communicated with and RBO in markets represented may be assigned this duty.

The Marketing Dictionary

Order Form—Provided for buyers by larger and medium size stores and chain stores; provides all necessary protection for buyers; generally made out in triplicate.

Ordinary Dating—A term of sale requiring that the invoice be paid within a specified number of days from the date of the invoice.

Organization—That management endeavors to achieve its objectives by direction the efforts of the people under its supervision.

Organizational Structure—Framework within which management can adequately control, supervise, delegate, and fix responsibilities, and synchronize the work done by divisions, departments, and individuals.

Orientation—All new employees in most department stores must receive two or more days of orientation to familiarize them with physical store layout, store policies, and operations.

Original Cost Method of Inventory Valuation—Valuing an inventory at the cost price actually paid for the goods.

Other Income—Income from sources other than the sale of merchandise. Such sources include, among others, interest and dividends received, and profits from the redeeming of securities.

Outfit Salescheck—Salescheck itemizing all units of customer's purchase.

Out of Stock—Lack of merchandise in store in styles, colors, material content, price lines customers want when they want it.

Outpost Displays—Merchandise displayed with informative signs, at traffic points away from its regular selling department.

Outstanding Orders—The amount of merchandise that a store or department has contracted for delivery during a period but has not yet received.

Overage—The difference between the book and physical inventories when the latter is the larger. Nearly all overages are caused by clerical errors.

Over-Exposure—Location of merchandise in areas where it cannot be watched or guarded by store personnel. Especially dangerous when a shoplifting program is noticeable in the store.

Overhead—A synonym for fixed expenses. The term is sometimes used interchangeably with total expense but this use is to be discouraged.

Over or Short—Resulting difference between established sales figure and actual audited figure, often caused by errors in change or missing saleschecks.

Over-the-Counter—A market for securities made up of securities dealers who may or may not be members of a securities exchange. Over-the-counter is mainly a market made over the telephone. Thousands of companies have insufficient shares outstanding, stockholders, or earnings to warrant application for listing on a stock exchange. Others may simply prefer not to list their securities of these companies are traded in the over-the-counter market between dealers for customers. The over-the-counter market is the chief market for U.S. Government bonds, municipal bonds, and bank and insurance stocks.

Package Delivery—Smaller packages of merchandise dispatched to customers through store's own delivery system or through cooperative or commercial company.

Paper Profit—The capital gain an investor would receive if he were to sell stocks he owns.

Parking Garages—Downtown multi-ramp garages within reasonable walking distance of store; in shopping centers because of high realestate costs and distance from stores, some centers are already constructing muti-ramp parking facilities.

Participating Preferred Stock—The owners of this stock are allowed to share in the excess earnings of a corporation.

Partnership—A form of business whereby two or more persons agree to share the risks and profits of operating the business. The issuing of stock, as with a corporation, is not involved.

Par Value—Stated monetary value printed on the face of preferred stock.

Payroll Expenses %—The total payroll for the work center expressed as a per cent of the total sales. The sales are the store sales where the center services the store but where the selling department is regarded as a work center, the sales are the department sales.

Peak Season—Months or season in which an item or line of merchandise is in greatest customer demand. Examples: skis during major snow months.

Penny Stocks—Low-priced issues often highly speculative selling at less than $1 a share. Frequently used as an uncomplimentary tern although a few penny stocks have developed into investment-caliber issues.

Permanent Press—A process applied by manufacturers to garments and domestics whereby merchandise requires no ironing or pressing, considered very important by customers.

Perpetual Inventory—A book inventory kept in continuous agreement with stock on hand by means of a detailed record that may also serve as a subsidiary ledger where dollar amounts as well as physical quantities are maintained. Sections of the stockroom are inventoried at short intervals and the quantities or amounts or both are adjusted, where necessary, to the physical count.

Personal Care Items—Hair dryers, electric shavers, saunas, electric hair curlers, hair setters, electric manicure and pedicure sets; merchandise to help improve customer's appearance.

Perpetual Inventory Method of Classification Control—The determination of the dollar inventories within each classification from daily sales and purchase records.

Physical Depreciation—Loss of usefulness in a fixed asset attributable to purely physical causes; wear and tear.

Physical inventory at Cost—The value of an inventory at aggregate cost prices.

Physical Inventory at Retail—The value of an inventory at aggregate retail prices.

Physical Inventory System of Unit Control—A system of stock control whereby the stock is counted at periodic intervals and the unit sales are derived from the inventory and purchase data.

Periodic Inventory Method of Classification Control—The determination of sales data within each merchandise classification from periodic counts of the inventory on hand.

Physical Inventory—An inventory determined by observation and evidenced by a listing of the actual count, weight or measure.

Physical Life—Total potential operating life, as a machine, as contrasted with economic life which may be much less because of the presence of obsolescence or inadequacy, or with.

Pick-Ups—Merchandise picked up from customer's home and returned to store by delivery department upon customer's request.

The Marketing Dictionary

Piece Goods—Fabrics from home sewing including woolens, cottons, synthetics.

Piggyback Freight—Goods are loaded on trucks which, in turn, are driven up onto special railroad flat cars. These cars are then made a part of a train moving in the direction of the trucks destinations, frequently overnight. Later at a predetermined point, the trucks are driven off the cars and proceed under their own power to their destination points.

Place Utility—To have the goods where they are wanted.

Planned Purchases—The amount of merchandise that may be received into stock during a period in order to "land" the stock at the end of the month at a predetermined figure Purchases may be planned in terms of retail value, cost value, or units. For control purposes, the first is the most common.

Plus Business—Selling merchandise or services over and above that normally expected.

Point-of-Purchase Displays—The use of packaging and store displays as a selling medium.

Portfolio—Securities owned by an individual or institution. A portfolio may contain bonds, preferred stocks, and common stocks of various types of enterprises.

Postage-Stamp Pricing—When it is desired that the final retail price of a product be identical nationally, the manufacturer must quote identical delivered prices throughout the market. This means that each buyer is charged an average freight cost, regardless of his location. This quotation of delivered prices on a uniform basis, with the seller paying the freight, reduces the yield to the seller as transportation charges mount. It is most common with items where transportation is a minor cost and where the advertising of prices on a national basis is usual.

Pot Shotting—A special promotion developing usually quick and important results.

Pre-Authorizing—Obtaining credit authorization for charge-send transactions prior to packages or merchandise leaving department.

Prediction—To tell in advance; prophecy as to probable success or failure of a plan or the probable success or failure of a marketing program. However, because an idea or product has will not be accepted today.

Preferred Resource—Manufacturer, wholesaler, or importer from which store buys important portion of a line or classification of merchandise and to whom store gives preferred treatment.

Preferred Stock—A class of stock with a claim on the company's earnings before dividends may be paid on the common stock. It usually has priority over common stocks if the company goes out of business. It is usually entitled to dividends at a specified rate.

Pre-Marketing or Pre-Ticketing—Marking of merchandise by manufacturer.

Pre-Packaging—Merchandise packaged by vendor for display, for "take-with" by customer or delivery by store. (Vendor can pre-package more economically via assembly line method than store.)

Prepaid Transportation—Cost of transportation of merchandise to store paid by resource. (When cost is paid by store, this expense muse be added to cost of merchandise in calculating markon.)

Prepay—Payment of all shipping charges for merchandise by vendor, who rebills charges to purchaser on invoice for the merchandise.

Preprint—Copy of an advertisement distributed to a store's customers and/or resources prior to publication in a general medium.

The Marketing Dictionary

Pre-Retailing—System in which all merchandise is purchased to or carried at a pre-determined price, which is on record in the receiving and marking room. (Ready-to-wear is generally an exception due to re-appraise value upon receipt in store.)

Pre-sold Merchandise—Where vendor's national advertising in magazines, newspapers, and via T.V. and radio create customer acceptance and in-store demand.

Pre-Ticketed—Merchandise priced by vendor either on package or on price tickets or tags (often supplied by store to vendor with season letter, price, other necessary information) prior to packing for shipment to store. This saves store time, effort, and money in getting merchandise through receiving and marking room and into selling floor.

Pre-Wrap—Wrapping of merchandise before putting on sale (finding extensive use for types of merchandise of standard quality); also, merchandise wrapped or packaged by manufacturer for store "send" or customer "take-with".

Price Brackets—Definite price zones or levels at which greatest sales volume can be produced.

Price Cutting—1)Cutting prices below a minimum resale price fixed (or suggested) by the vendor, and 2) selling below cost or below cost plus expenses of doing business; many discounters have developed a customer following by price cutting, particularly on nationally known brands.

Price Leader—An item of merchandise priced abnormally low for the purpose of attracting customers—a device employed by retail stores to increase sales of other products, and employed by manufacturers and distributors to attract attention to their brand and increase sales of other items. The practice runs some risk of violation Federal Law. Less diversified competitors are particularly vulnerable to such competition, their survival being dependent on a normal margin on the price-leader item.

Price Levels—Same as Price Brackets.

Price Line—A specific price at which a representative stock assortment is carried.

Price Zone—A range of prices all appealing to customers in a certain income group.

Pricing Policy—The body of principles followed over a period of time by the management of a business enterprise in fixing the selling price of its product or service. After deciding upon his basic price through an analysis of costs and market expectations, a manufacturer immediately faces the problems of creating a price system or price policies. Decisions must be made about freight charges, methods of distribution, discounts, and similar policies. Each of these involves pricing.

Primary Advertising—Intended to stimulate an interest in and a desire for a certain class of goods, particularly for some new type of product that has just come onto the market, or I which the public has yet to manifest any appreciable interest.

Principal—The person for whom a broker executes an order. When a dealer buys or sells for his own account, he deals as a principal. The term "principal" may also refer to a person's capital or to the face amount of a bond.

Private Brand—Controlled or private-label merchandise developed under store's own brand or developed under RBO's label exclusively for member stores.

The Marketing Dictionary

Private Corporation—One chartered, owned, and operated by individuals either for the profit of its owners or for social, charitable, or educational purposes.

Procurement Function—Buying merchandise for resale to store's customers.

Product Duplication—Similar or actual duplication of exact products from two or more resources: frequently increases store's inventory unnecessarily and confuses customer's selection.

Production—The making of goods or providing of services for human use.

Productivity—The output of the workload per manhour. It is found by dividing the workload by the number of manhours required to handle the load.

Product Mix—Adjustment of the product line so that the market is best served.

Profit—The excess of revenue, proceeds or selling price over related costs; any pecuniary benefit arising from a commercial operation, from the practice of a profession, or from one or more individual transactions of any person.

Profit Corporation—A privately-owned business, using the corporate form, that operates to make profits for its shareholders.

Profit Sharing—An incentive program in which a firm's profits are distributed to its employees without them having to buy stock in the company.

Profit Squeeze—Generally caused by increased wholesale costs, plus selling costs, that cannot be passed onto store's customer; or by severe competition from other retail stores.

Programmed Merchandising—Advance sales and promotion planning executed to produce predetermined profits.

Programming—In computer language, instructions given a computer, what the electronic device is to do and produce.

Promissory Note—A note showing evidence of borrowing. It is signed by a borrower, and held by the lender. It states the amount and terms of repayment and interest, if any.

Promotional Allowances—An amount granted to the store by the seller of merchandise to cover all or part of the store's cost of advertising or otherwise promoting the sale of the merchandise to the consumer. When the store is allowed to deduct the allowance from the face of the invoice without giving any assurance that it will us the allowance, the allowance is simply a form of trace or quantity discount. Otherwise it may be treated as a credit to promotional expense and not be credited to the cost of the merchandise.

Promotional Kit—Ideas, suggestions, materials supplied to store by vendor, whether manufacturer, importer, or wholesaler.

Proportionally Equal Terms—Vendor's dealings with all customers on uniform basis regardless of size.

Proprietorship—A business conducted by a single owner.

Prorated Expenses—Joint expenses that cannot be charged directly to selling departments nor allocated to them on a basis that measures the service each has received. They are assigned to selling departments prorate to dollar sales volume.

Prospectus—A circular which describes securities being offered for sale to the public and contains certain other information required by the Federal Securities Act of 1933.

The Marketing Dictionary

Proximo—(specified date in the coming month) Terms 2/10 prox. require payment on the 10th of the month following purchase to secure the 2 percent discount. Actually such terms are the equivalent of 2/10 EOM.

Proxy—Written authorization given by a shareholder to someone else to represent him and vote his shares at a shareowner's meeting.

Publicity—Any form of commercially significant news about a product, an institution, a service, or a person published in space or radio time that is not paid for the sponsor.

Publicity Director—Sometimes called "Sales Promotion Manager." In large retail store supervises advertising, display, special activities or events, press and/or public relations or events, press and/or public relations managers and frequently the fashion coordinator and comparison shoppers. In medium-size store, managers may report directly to general merchandise manager. In small store, advertising manager may do everything in publicity and promotion.

Pulling-Out-All-Stops—Utilizing all available promotional media plus intensified departmental selling efforts.

Purchase—An outlay for property or service; the property or service acquired.

Purchase Order—A document authorizing a vendor to deliver described merchandise or materials at a specified price. Upon acceptance by a vendor, a purchase order becomes a contract. Several copies of a purchase order are customarily prepared.

Purchases—The amount of merchandise received by a retailer during a period. The term is distinguished from orders that represent the amount contracted for delivery during a period but not necessarily received in that period.

Purchasing Agents—Executive who purchases products for store maintenance and operation—not for resale to customers.

Purchasing Agent Store—A selection or purchasing agent where major emphasis is placed on selecting the right merchandise for its customers and on maintaining assortments.

Purchasing Power—The ability to buy; hence (a) the quantity of a particular class of goods or services that may be purchased for a given sum of money, such as one dollar, or (b) the percentage relationship of such a quantity to that so purchasable at some preceding point of time.

Quantity Discount—An allowance given by a seller to a purchaser because of the size of an individual purchase transaction. This practice is not in violation of Federal laws dealing with price discrimination provided the allowance granted represents a saving in selling costs. It is sometimes justified on the ground that the seller in good faith must meet a competitor's price. Legal restriction on dual pricing serves the purpose of preventing large buyers from taking advantage of their bargaining power to reduce acquisition costs, and to reflect these savings in lower resale prices: competition that smaller firms could not meet. While it (is) argued that this restriction is detrimental to consumers, there is no certainty that, if small firms are eliminated by price competition, large firms would continue to pass on such savings to consumers.

Quota—Figure establishing goal of daily or weekly sales to be obtained by salespeople, individually or by department.

Quota Bonus—Additional salary or commission paid for attaining or exceeding established quota.

Rate of Exchange—The number of dollars or cents exchangeable for a unit of foreign currency at a given time.

Rate of Productivity—The amount of goods or services produced by each worker each hour, (or, per minute, per day, per week, etc.). For example: if 1,000 workers turn out 1,000 pairs of shoes each hour, the rate of productivity is one pair of shoes per man per hour.

Rate-of-Return Pricing—A method of determining prices by adding a markup on costs which will produce a predetermined return on investment.

Ratio—This term refers to the various analyses made by a money, or credit lending agency of the financial statements of a given individual, company, or other business enterprise seeking credit to determine the feasibility of granting the requested credit.

Raw Data—Information fed into computer usually by punched tape or cards or, increasingly, by computer's scanning or reading original documents.

Raw Materials—Those industrial goods which in part or in whole become a portion of the physical product but which have undergone no more processing than is required for convenience, protection, or economy in storage, transportation, or handling.

Reactivating of Inactive Charge Customers—A promotional program developed to induce former charge customers to make use of their charge accounts.

Real Capital—Equipment, machines, buildings, etc., used in production and paid for by money capital.

Real Estate Manager—Executive in charge of land and buildings occupied by store-flagship, branch stores, warehouses, service buildings.

Real Estate Subsidiary—Owning and/or operating property, such as store's owning an entire shopping center, leasing space to other stores.

Realignment of Buyer Functions—With development of branch stores, responsibilities and duties of the buyer are changing from procurement and departmental personnel purchasing, allocation of merchandise of flagship and branch stores.

Rebate—An allowance; a deduction; a refund of a part of the price paid for a good or service.

ROG or AOG (Receipt of Goods: Arrival of Goods) Dating—Under these terms, the discount period is based on the date on which the purchaser receives the goods. For example, merchandise with a 2/10, n/30, ROG dating terms are employed to meet objections of distant purchasers who would be at a disadvantage if terms were based on "date of invoice." A supplier located in the east with customers throughout the nation, must, of necessity, employ ROG terms if he is to meet competition from the customer's local suppliers; otherwise, if date of invoice prevailed, a purchaser located a short distance from the eastern supplier would have a chance to receive goods and even sell some before making payment while the distant customer might have to pay for the merchandise long before it was received. The benefits of ROG terms are enjoyed by the purchaser only when the bill is discounted. If the bill is not paid in time to take the discount, the net period is measured from the date of the invoice.

Receipt of Goods—Terms: Cash discount terms that begin when merchandise reaches store (designed to benefit retailers far from resource; also permits check of goods prior to due date for discount).

Receiving—Process of accepting new merchandise at store or warehouse; includes initiating paperwork to get merchandise "on the books" and processing incoming transportation bills.

Receiving and Marking Manager—Is in charge of merchandise, routing it to warehouse, forward stock, flagship selling floor, or each branch store as directed by buyer.

Receiving Apron—Form attached to store's purchase order contains information concerning status of vendor's shipment; forwarded by receiving department to invoice office, which audits all invoices before bills are paid.

Recession—A period of slow-down in economic activity marked by a reduction in production, sales, profit, employment, and sometimes prices. Not as severe as a depression.

Reciprocal Buying—Favoring customers over prospective vendors who are not customers when purchase orders are placed.

Refer—Applied to customer's account when its status is in doubt; credit authorizer then refers it to supervisor or credit manager.

Refund Check—Form for refund of amount of purchase on a customer return; also, a bank check sent to customer as refund for merchandise returned.

Regional Center for Chain—Where a retail organization establishes several stores in a metromarket in order to justify local warehousing, merchandising and advertising expenses.

Regional Shopping Center—50 to 100 stores, including at least one major department store branch; 35 or more acres; requiring trading area of 100,000 people to support it, usually over 200,000 square feet in store area.

Regional Stores—Branch store generally situated at considerable distance from central downtown or flagship store, operating under name of parent store (its merchandise is frequently operated on regional store's own merchandising staff), frequently operated on autonomous basis.

Regular Account—Conventional charge account billed each month and to be paid during ensuing 30 days.

Rehabilitation—Renovation and modernization of a physical store.

Relative Workload—The amount of workload incident to $100 of total sales. It is found by dividing the workload by the sales in units of $100.

Remote Delivery—Routing of merchandise from main metropolitan warehouse to distant customers by way of regional delivery stations in suburbs, or by trucks direct from store or warehouse.

Renegotiation—The procedure, followed by governmental agencies, often leading to the adjustment of a contract price or a contract amount after delivery has been made and the profit derived from the contract has been determined.

Reorder Period—The frequency planned for reordering a specific item.

Repeated Event—Reordering and advertising of more merchandise, as a repeated event, when special price sale or advantageous buy has been advertised and sold out quickly.

Replacement Cost or Value—The cost at current prices, in a particular locality or market area, of replacing an item of property or of a group of assets.

Replenishment Orders—To fill-in assortments in a specific classification; usually referred to as a reorder.

Reprint—Copy of an advertisement distributed to a store's customers and/or resources following publication in a general media.

Rep (short for representative)—Individuals or wholesale companies representing vendors or a manufacturer in specified sales territory who solicit and accept orders that are shipped from vendor's factory or distributing point, but who do not actually own or stock merchandise.

Requisition System of Expense Control—A system of authorizing expenditures for expense items only after an outlay has been requested in writing and has been checked against the budgeted figure for that type of outlay.

Research—In business, the search for new and better products or ways of producing, marketing, packaging, etc., In securities, it is the task of seeking the facts about companies so as to enable investors to make intelligent decisions.

Research Director—Responsible for all research activities in store operation and customer research (becoming increasingly important).

Reserve Requisition Control—A unit control system whereby all requisitions from reserve to forward stock are treated as sales.

Reserve Stock Control—Method of earmarking sufficient amount of stock to maintain business while additional stock is purchased.

Resident Buying Office—Represents the store at the main manufacturing centers. Duties include buying, studying market conditions, and analyzing trends in styles.

Resource—A manufacturer, importer, wholesaler, distributor, selling agent, rack jobber from whom a store buys or accepts merchandise as owner or on selling consignment.

Retail—The price at which goods are offered for sale. In practice, three different retail prices may be recognized: 1) the original retail price placed on goods when first purchased; 2) the current retail price of goods in stock, which may be more or less than the original retail if the price has been changed;

and 3) the sales retail, the price as which the sale is actually made, after mark-downs, if any.

Retail Deals—Based on advertising and promotional allowances by vendors in addition to special deals or quantity purchase prices.

Retail Owned—Individual stores or cooperative chains owned by individuals, families, or partnerships.

Retail Deductions—The retail value that is subtracted from total merchandise handled at retail during a period. It consists of net sales plus retail reductions.

Retail Franchise—Exclusive Ownership by store in a trading area of prestige manufacturer's line; frequently a line selectively distributed.

Retailing—Basically the business of buying for resale to the ultimate customer; also known as "acting as the customer's agent".

Retail Merchandising—The planning done by retailers; 1) to achieve an assortment of merchandise that is balanced to customer demand and 2) to maintain a balance among the factors of sales volume, costs, and expenses that will both promote growth and provide a profit potential. In a broad sense, many use the term to denote the buying and selling activities of a merchant.

Retail Method Accounting—Accounting method in which all percentages are relative to retail price instead of cost price. In cost method of accounting all percentages are relative to the cost.

Retail Method (of inventory)—A method of maintaining a book inventory by which the cost of sales and inventories of department and other retail stores are determined at the close of intermediate accounting periods without a physical stocktaking. Generally, the method involves ascertaining the ratios between costs and selling prices of purchases, including the beginning inventory, and applying this percentage to net sales to obtain cost of sales. markons, markdowns, and revisions of both also enter into the computation. As in the case of any book inventory, a periodic physical verification is an invariable accompaniment. Under the retail method, physical inventories are valued at selling prices and reduced to cost by application of the computed percentage.

Retail Orientation—Knowledge of how retail stores are organized; how they actually operate; how to work successfully with them.

Retail Reductions—The difference between the aggregate original retail value of merchandise disposed of during a period and net sales. It is the sum of markdown, merchandise shortage, and discounts to employees and customers.

Retail Sales—Sales by retail outlets, such as stores, shops, etc. The trend of retail sales, up or down, is an important indication of economic vitality.

Retained Earnings—Money from profits left to corporations after paying taxes and dividends. This is generally capital used for expansion or increasing efficiency of production.

Return—[See Yield]

Revenue—Money received by government from taxes; also, income from investments.

Return Policy—Rules and regulations formulated by store's manager covering merchandise returns by customers including exchange, credit, cash, refunds, adjustments.

Returns from Customers—Cancellation of Sales. The returns for a period measured by the retail value of goods returned by customers to the store and returned to stock. Even exchanges in which a customer returns one article for another of the same value, are usually not included in either gross sales or returns. Uneven exchanges, however, are generally included in gross sales and in returns.

Returns to Vendor—Shipments of merchandise returned by store to vendor because of errors in filling store's purchase order, substitutions in shipment, late delivery, defective materials or workmanship to fit, or other breaches of contract.

Revision of Retail Downward—A decrease in price that is subtracted from the retail purchase figure before the markup percent is calculated. It includes additional markup cancellations, corrections of clerical errors in recording and pricing retail purchases, and retail price reductions growing out of rebate (allowance) from the manufacturer. markdowns are not included in revisions.

Rights—When a company wants to raise more funds by issuing additional stock, it may give its stockholders the opportunity, ahead of others, to buy the new stock in proportion to the number of shares each owns. The piece of paper evidencing this privilege is called a right or warrant. Because the additional stock is usually offered to stockholders below the current market price, rights ordinarily have a market value of their own and are actively traded. In most cases they must be exercised within a relatively short period. Failure to exercise or sell rights may result in actual loss to the holder.

Role—Refers to the duties and obligations implicit in a job.

Round Lot—A unit of trading or a multiple thereof. On the New York Stock Exchange the unit of trading is generally 100 shares in stocks, although in some stocks it is 10.

The Marketing Dictionary

Round-the-Corner Service—Provided by wholesaler or distribution, who provides immediate delivery of merchandise in contrast to manufacturer, who ships from distant factory or regional warehouse.

Routine—A program or section of a program consisting of a set of sequence of coded instructions used to direct a computer in performing a sequence of operations.

Routing Instructions—Provided by store to be attached by buyer to purchase order, informing vendor of routing and shipping instructions, specifying types of transportation store wants merchandise shipped by.

Rub Off—Secondary benefit by a department from a promotion in another department. Example: Opportunities for sales of oversize bed sheets, blankets, comforters, bedspreads, because of sale of king or queen size mattresses and box springs.

Runner—Item that sells and sells (everybody's sweetheart); also used for messenger.

Rural Oriented—Stores who merchandise and promotional staffs are knowledgeable as to types, quality, and price lines rural customers will order by mail..

Safety Factor—A reserve for contingencies, especially for unforeseen increases in rate of sale. It may be expressed in terms of weeks supply or as a specific quantity in units. When applied to a classification rather than a single item of merchandise, it also must include a provision for a basic assortment of colors, sizes, and so forth. Also called reserve.

Sale—A business transaction involving the delivery (i.e., the giving) of a commodity, an item of merchandise or property, a right, or a service, in exchange for (the receipt of) cash, a promise to pay, or money equivalent, or for any combination of these items; it is recorded and reported in terms of the amount of such cash, promise to pay, or money equivalent.

Sales—The amounts received or accrued to the store in exchange for merchandise sold to customers during an account period.

Sales Analysis—That part of sales audit which provides totals of sales by salespeople, departments, classifications, etc.

Sales Analysis system of Unit Control—A system of stock control by which the sales are analyzed in units as they occur by such factors as, classification, price line, materials, color, size, and style number. A perpetual inventory system is often maintained.

Sales Audits—Work for checking media from selling floor for purpose of control, reporting, accounting.

Sales Budget—An estimate of the probable dollar sales and probable selling costs for a specified period.

Comment: The use of the term is sometimes confined to an estimate of future sales. This does not conform to the general use of the term budget which includes schedules of both receipts and expenditures. If the sales budget is to be used as a device to facilitate sales control and management, it should include the probably cost of getting the estimated volume of sales. The failure to allow proper weight to this item in their calculations is one of the most consistently persistent and fatal mistakes made by American business concerns. It has led to much of the striving after unprofitable volume that has been so costly.

Sales check—Form in triplicate listing customer's purchases, including price.

Sales Disposal—System in which sales person disposes of entire transaction including wrapping of merchandise (there is a trend to this operation).

Sales Forecast—An estimate of dollar or unit sales for a specified future period under a proposed marketing plan or program. The forecast may be for a specified item of merchandise or for an entire line; it may be for a market as a whole or for any portion thereof.

Comment: Two sets of factors are involved in making a sales forecast 1) those forces outside the control of the firm of which the forecast is made that are likely to influence its sales. and 2) changes in the marketing methods or practices of the firm that are likely to affect its sales. In the course of planning future activities the management of a given firm may make several sales forecasts, each consisting of an estimate of probable sales if a given marketing plan is adopted or a given set of outside forces prevails. The estimated effects on sales of a number of marketing plans may be computed in the process of arriving at that marketing program which will, in the opinion of the officials of the company, be best designed to promote its welfare.

Sales Manager—Some larger stores are placing responsibility for personal selling efforts, for supervision and on-the-floor training of salespersons as well as point-of-purchase signing and demonstrations with a sales manager. Salespeople report to him or his assistants rather than to buyers.

Sales Plan—Department's promotional program for 6-month period, subject to monthly revision to take advantage of opportunistic purchases and other unpredictable merchandising opportunities.

Sales Planning—The work of setting up objectives for marketing activity and of determining and scheduling the steps necessary to achieve such objectives.

Comment: This term includes not only the work of deciding upon the goals or results to be attained through marketing activity, but also the determination in detail of exactly how they are to be accomplished. The result of this work is a Sales Plan.

Sales Potential—The share of a market potential which a company expects to achieve.

Comment: The portion of the total expected sales of an industry which the managers of a firm expect that firm to get is the Sales Potential for that firm. By means of marketing research a firm may establish a market potential for the industry of which it is a part. Through the use of one or more sales forecasts its managers may determine upon a sales potential for the firm. From this may be derived the sales budget and a sales quota for the entire company or any part of it.

Sales Promotion—Activities which assist in the sale and advertising of goods.

Sales Supporting Staff—Personnel Closely allied to selling activities but not engaged in making sales to customers, includes operations who support merchandising and selling staffs.

Sales System—Method by which transaction with customer is recorded.

Sales Training Director—Responsible for training all sales personnel in the technical aspects of selling operation; reviews vendor's salesman's sales-meeting agendas; review vendor's slide or movie presentations to eliminate those that downgrade competitive products, particularly private brands, and to make certain presentation will assist salespeople in selling the classification of merchandise concerned.

The Marketing Dictionary

Sales Quota—A sales goal assigned to a marketing unit for use in the management of sales efforts. It applies to a specified period and may be expressed in dollars or in physical units.

Comment: The quota may be used in checking the efficiency, stimulating the efforts, or in fixing the payment of individual salesmen or groups of salesmen or other personnel engaged in sales work. A quota may be for a salesman, a territory, a branch house, or for the company as a whole. It may be different from the sales figure set up in the sales budget. Since it is a managerial device, it is not an immutable figure inexorably arrived at by the application of absolutely exact statistical formulas, but may be set up with an eye to its psychological effects upon the sales personnel or any part of it. Two salesmen, working in territories of identical potentials, may be assigned different quotas in accordance with the anticipated effects of this variation on their sales efforts because of differences in their characters or personalities.

Sale Value—The price at which an asset of any kind can be sold, less whatever cost is yet to be incurred: a basis sometimes referred to in the valuation of inventories.

Salon—Shop where higher-priced apparel and corresponding accessories are sold.

Salvage—Applied to merchandise soiled beyond reclamation for salable purposes that must be disposed of through other channels; also refers to re-usable wrapping materials.

Sample room—Areas in store or in RBO where vendor salesmen display merchandise samples to buyers or market representative.

Savings and Loan Association—Formed for two major purposes: (a) to loan money for the purchase of homes and business properties, and (b) to enable individuals to invest funds with comparative safety at yields usually higher than available in savings accounts with banks.

Savings Bank—Accept deposits from savers on which an announced rate of interest is paid.

Scarcity (economics)—A condition of insufficiency to supply all levels of demands; said of any economic good, or (of) a good which requires economizing.

Seal of Approval—Intended to identify goods that are outstanding. Emanating from such organizations as Good Housekeeping, etc.

Seasonal Employees—Personnel employed during peak selling periods such as pre-Christmas, Easter, and for store-wide sales events.

Seasonal Merchandise—Merchandise purchased to meet demands or specific seasons (extreme instances: purchases for summer and winter clothing, outdoor furniture.)

Season Letter—Code assigned to merchandise received during 6-month spring or fall season that indicates age of stock.

Seat—A traditional figure of speech for a membership on a securities or commodity exchange. The price of a membership reflects supply and demand.

Secondary Price Line—A price line at which a lesser assortment is carried but one which is adequate to meet the requirements of a typical customer.

Section Manager—Executive in operating division as management representative with disciplinary and adjustment jurisdiction, budgeting and staffing responsibility within departments under his supervision.

Secured Account—Any account against which collateral or other security is held.

The Marketing Dictionary

Secured Creditor—A person whose claim against another is protected by collateral or by a mortgage or other lien; is the protection is ample the claim is designated as "fully secured"; if the protection is not complete, the claim is designated as "partially secured."

Securities—Stocks and bonds, etc.

SEC—The Securities and Exchange Commission, an administrative agency of the Federal Government. The SEC administers the Securities Act of 1933, the Securities Exchange Act of 1934, the Trust Indenture Act, the Investment Company Act, and the Public Utility Holding Company Act.

Security Exchange—An organization that provides facilities for its members to buy and sell securities. Also called a stock exchange.

Segment—One of the parts into which something naturally separates or divides: classifications within a selling department.

Segmented Merchandising—Merchandising for and appealing to specific age groups or other groups or other groups with common interests.

Selection vs. Corporation—Two major responsibilities of buyers, which vary with nature of goods to be merchandised. Example: In dress department, buying or ability to select wisely is perhaps 90% of the job; in drug department, operation is 90% meaning ability to analyze and plan operations ahead and so to manipulate volume, markon, and expenses as to yield a profit.

Selective Advertising—Supposed to impel consumers toward the purchase of a particular brand of goods.

Selective Selling—The policy of selling only to dealers and distributors who meet the seller's requirements, such as size of orders, volume of purchases, profitability, or area or type of operations.

Comment: While accounts are selected on a variety of bases, probably the most common are size and the kind and amount of reselling service the account is willing and able to give to the goods or services of the seller. Possibly the soundest basis is that of the amount of potential net profit to be derived from the business placed by the account.

Selling Agent—Independent business enterprises operating on a commission basis, whose principal function is to sell the entire output of a given line of goods for one or more manufacturers with whom they maintain continuous contractual relationship.

Selling Area—That part of sales floor devoted exclusively to selling (shoe and ready-to-wear stock rooms, fitting rooms, and wrapping stations are considered part of selling area when sale could not be consummated without them).

Selling Cost—Any expense or class of expense incurred in selling or marketing.

Selling Days—Number of days per month or week that store is open; after refers to period between Thanksgiving Day and Christmas Day.

Selling Department—A physical division of a store, containing related merchandise grouped for purposes of 1) determining the operation profit for each grouping; 2) controlling buying and pricing more exactly; and 3) promoting sales more effectively.

Selling Expenses—Those that are incurred as a direct result of the sales activities of the firm.

"Send" Transactions—Customer purchases to be delivered by store versus "take-withs" where customers personally carries merchandise from store. "Sends" are greater from flagship store than from branch stores.

The Marketing Dictionary

Separation of Authority—Definite spellout of an individual's authority, responsibilities and duties.

Service Area—That part of sales floor devoted to servicing the selling area (such as escalators, elevators, stairways, freight landings, rest rooms, show windows)

Service Building—Building remote downtown store used for delivery purposes, repair facilities, workrooms for larger merchandise, warehousing.

Service Building Superintendent—Individual in charge of and responsible for operation of services such as refinishing furniture, floor coverings, drapery and upholstery workrooms, ready-to-wear alterations and building.

Service Center—An area frequently near small electronics department, however, may be located in warehouse where repairs or alterations are made.

Service Mix—Determination of service and quantity policies so as to produce the desired customer satisfaction.

Services—Activities or anticipated satisfactions which are offered for sale either as such or in connection with the sale of goods. Examples are amusements, hotel service, electric service, transportation, the services of barber shops and beauty shops, repair and maintenance service, the work of credit rating bureaus. This list is merely illustrative and no attempt has been made to make it complete. The term also applies to the various activities, such as credit extension, service and help of salespeople, delivery, by which the seller serves the convenience of his customers.

Service Shopper—Special salesperson designated to accompany customers who plan purchases in a number of departments.

Service Superintendent—Senior management executive in complete charge of all customer services.

Shareholder—Also known as a stockholder. He owns part of a corporation by buying stock in it.

Share of Market—Percent of a metro-market sales volume attained by a store, a department, or a classification within a department in the store.

Shareowner—Anyone who owns one or more shares of stock in a corporation.

Shoplifting—Stealing of store's merchandise by customers. Of growing concern to all types of retailers.

Shopping Goods—Those consumers' goods which the customer in the process of selection and purchase characteristically compares on such bases as suitability, quality, price and style. Examples of goods that most consumers probably buy as shopping goods are: millinery, furniture, dress goods, men's and women's ready-to-wear, shoes, jewelry, and residential real estate (not bought for purposes of speculation).

Comment: It should be emphasized that a given article may be bought by one customer as a shopping good and buy another as a speciality or convenience good. The general classification depends upon the way in which the average or typical buyer purchases.

Shortage—The difference between the book and the physical inventory, when the former is the larger. It may be calculated at cost or retail value or in terms of units. It represents 1) clerical errors in calculating the book and/or physical inventories, and 2) physical merchandise losses, caused by such factors as theft, breakage, and charging customers for less merchandise than is actually delivered to them.

Short Merchandise—Merchandise purchased in limited quantities, generally in extreme sizes, to fill an assortment; also, items of purchase that through error were not included in customer's package or were missing in shipment from vendor.

Short SKU—System which permits full identification of an item, making possible the use of source-marked tickets either for backroom processing or cash register input, so that ultimately a store will be able to count sales, not stocks.

Short Supply Situation—Merchandise where buyer has difficulty in maintaining adequate supply.

Showrooms—Spaces maintained in various cities by vendor-manufacturers, importers, wholesalers is displayed for store buyers and merchandise managers to select styles and place orders.

Shrinkage—Difference (on minus side) between merchandise on hand shown by physical inventory and that shown as "book value".

Side-Line Stores—Stores run by organizations whose main activity is other than retailing.

Single-Line Store—Small, independently owned, that carries a single line of merchandise, such as food, hardware, drugs, millinery, or men's furnishings.

Single Posting—One-time posting of customer's purchases to the statement, which is used as a ledger sheet (in this instance, saleschecks are photographed on microfilm and filed for reference in adjustments).

Sister Stores—Member stores of a resident buying office. (The Dayton Company; the J.L. Hudson Company). Stores owned by a corporation (Jordan Marsh, Boston; Jodan Marsh, Florida).

Sitdown Strike—Workers appear at their posts but refuse to perform their appointed tasks or to leave the premises until their demands are met.

Site Saturation—A condition where a given location offers little, if any, opportunity for future expansion.

Size Lining—Method of organizing or grouping merchandise for selling by size. (Example: dress department set up with dresses of all colors, types, prices, and identified as "Size 10-20", "Size 38-44", etc.)

SKU (Stock Keeping Unit)—Represents item of merchandise which is in stock.

Sleeper—Potential "hot item" that, with aggressive promotion, may be developed into a runner.

Slowdown Strike—Workers continue to work but at a markedly reduced tempo so that production is curtailed but not completely halted.

Small Wares—Term applied to general articles of merchandise, usually found on main floor of department stores.

Soft Goods—Ready-to-wear for women, children, men, fashion accessories, piece goods, domestics.

Software—General purpose programs, normally furnished by EPD equipment manufacturers, for use in extending the capabilities and functions of the basic computer.

Soleplate—A plate upon which another product is placed; i.e., to protect a table top or counter from the heat of a small electrical appliance.

Sorter—Personnel in audit department who sort saleschecks, collate by kind of sale, inspect for missing saleschecks, also applied to collector of customers' names in cycle billing; also, sorter of packages for delivery routes.

Source Marking—Pre-ticketing by resource before shipment. Very important in expediting arrival of merchandise on selling floor because not held up in receiving for price ticketing by store and also, less expensive because merchandise does not have to be opened in receiving, ticketed, then repackaged.

Special Account—Account used for special purposes or for extraordinary means of payment.

Special Delivery—Delivery of package at certain time at specific request of customer.

Special Events Director—Reports to sales promotion manager; cooperates with advertising and display departments in activating promotions; supervises actual operation of special events.

Specialists—A person who devotes himself to one subject or to one particular branch or classification of a store's operation. Example: An individual who is devoted to handling via EPD or manually or both the production of merchandising and unit control data.

Special Orders—Readiness to procure for the customer anything not stocked.

Speciality Goods—The consumers' goods on which a significant group of buyers characteristically insist and for which they are willing to make a special purchasing effort. Examples of articles that are usually bought as speciality goods are: specific brands of fancy groceries, watches, men's shoes, and possibly automobiles.

Comment: There seems to be room for considerable doubt as to whether the distinction between Shopping Goods and Speciality Goods is any longer valid and useful. There is less doubt of the validity of the class, Shopping Goods, than of Speciality Goods.

Speciality Salesman—A salesman, other than retail, who specializes in the sale of one product or a few products of a seller's line.

Speciality Shop—Confines itself to a small segment of the merchandise in any single category, usually in the apparel field.

Speciality Stores—Stores concentrating on specific classifications of merchandise. Examples: jewelry, women's apparel and accessories, shoes, intimate apparel, sporting goods.

Speciality Wholesaler—Carry limited or short lines in the areas in which they operate.

Specific Duty—A specific amount stated in dollars and cents per pound, gallon, bushel, or other unit of measurement levied against imported merchandise.

Speculation—The use of funds by a speculator.

Speculative Purchasing—Done to take advantage of the anticipated price rise. Purchasing departments buy in large quantities to take advantage of current low prices.

Speculator—One who is willing to assume a relatively large risk in the hope of gain. His principal concern is to increase his capital rather than his dividend income. The speculator may buy and sell the same day or speculate in an enterprise which he does not expect to be profitable for years.

Split—The division of the outstanding shares of a corporation into a larger number of shares. ! 3-for-1 split by a company with 1 million shares outstanding would result in 3 million shares outstanding. Each holder of 100 shares before the 3-for-1 split would have 300 shares, although his proportionate equity in the company would remain the same, since 100 parts of 1 million are the equivalent of 300 parts of 3 million. Ordinarily, splits must be voted by directors and approved by shareholders.

The Marketing Dictionary

Split Ticket—Price ticket perforated so portion can be removed for unit control purposes.

Spot Announcement—Short, frequently recorded commercials given on many different stations in the time between programs.

Spot Check—Inspection and count of small, random amount of goods in large shipments.

Spot Light—Light that concentrates rays on a specific area or object.

Spot Price—The price of a commodity available for immediate sale and delivery, the commodity being referred to as a spot commodity.

Spot Sale—The sale of a commodity to be immediately delivered, often on a cash basis.

Spot Shipments—Freight-car shipment with instructions to spot car at certain siding or at warehouse.

Standard of Living—The amount of goods, services, and cultural activities an individual, family or nation owns and makes use of. Also, the ease or comfort in which an individual or family lives.

Staple Stock—There is always the problem of overlap, in defining basic stock vs. staple stock. Essentially, the difference between basic and staple is assortment vs. single items. Staple stock is made up of items that are in practically continuous demand. Basic stock is an assortment of items that are in current demand. Basic stock includes stable stock items.

State Stuffer—National advertising with "where to buy it" identifications created for retail use, sized and weighted to fit customer bill envelopes and coincide with postage budget (not to be confused with direct mail).

Status—Derives from the manner in which one's superiors, equals, and subordinates regard the position occupied.

Stock—[See Common Stock and Preferred Stock]

Stock Alterations—The cost of altering and renovating goods in stock as distinct from goods ordered by customers. The cost of the work on stock is to be treated as a part of the cost purchase figure, not as a part of alteration and workroom costs.

Stock Book—Record of purchases from orders and of sales from stubs of price tickets usually maintained by buyer.

Stock Certificate—The piece of paper a shareowner receives which is evidence of his ownership of one or more shares of stock.

Stock Control—Broad term for various systems and methods to control stock; i.e., keep it in line with customer demand, one step ahead when demand goes up; slowed up when demand falters.

Stock Exchange—A place where stocks of approved companies are listed, and then may be bought and sold. The New York Stock Exchange, located in New York City, is the largest of the exchanges in the nation.

Stock-Sales Ratio—The ration between the retail stock at the first (or end) of the month and sales for that month. The B.O.M. stock-sales ratio is the dollar stock on the first of the month. The E.O.M. stock -sales ratio is the dollar stock at the end of the month divided by the sales for the month.

Stock Ticker—A machine which reports transactions in stock shortly after they occur on the floor of the exchange. Tickers are located in brokerage offices throughout the country.

Stock Turn—The ratio between sales and average inventory. It is calculated in any of the following ways: 1) Net sales , average inventory at retail; 2) Gross costs of goods sold , average inventory at cost; 3) number of units sold , average unit inventory.

The Marketing Dictionary

Stock-Turn Rate—The stock-turn for a period of one year.

Stop order—An order to buy or sell a stock when the price of the stock reaches, or sells through the price specified by the buyer or seller. A stop order may be used in an effort to protect a paper profit, or to try to limit a possible loss to a certain amount. Since it becomes a market order when the stop price is reached, there is no certainty that will be executed at that price. It is also called a stop loss order.

Store Division—Major group in a store. In merchandising, there are: piece goods and household textiles, small-wares, ready-to-wear accessories, women's and children's outer apparel, men's and boy' wear, home furnishings. Other store divisions include: controller, operation, sales promotion, personnel, and frequently in larger stores, branch-store division.

Store Network—Where flagship store with branches develops as a regional retail system beyond immediate metro-market.

Store's Own Brand (S.O.B.)—Store's private brand, presumably offers same quality and quantity for less money than national brands or greater quantity and equal quality for same money.

"Store's Store"—A retail operation that executives in other stores throughout the United States and Canada visit and watch because of superior operations that can be adapted by their sore.

Strike—Temporary refusal by employees to continue their work until their demands have been granted by management.

Stub—In merchandise control, second part of price ticket removed by sales-people at time of sale for unit merchandise-control.

Stub (Stubbing)—Extra copy of address label of salescheck which accompanies package to delivery depot, where it is removed and filed for use in adjustment of non-delivery complaints.

Style Piracy—Close copy, and sale at a lower price, of a manufacturer's original design by another manufacturer. It can be disaster or is for a store when a competitor offers copy at a lower price.

Subteens (Girls) Department—Separate RTM and accessories department appealing to girls from approximately 9 to 13 years old "who feel they are older than they will ever be again" and want to shop without their mothers (one of the fastest growing departments in a store).

Superettes—Small, self-service grocery stores. They may be former service stores that have been converted to self-service.

Supermarket—A departmentalized food store, with most departments on a self-service basis, having a minimum sales volume ranging from $375,000 to $1,000,000 per year.

Supplement of the Markup—The retail as a per cent of the cost. It is calculated as 100% plus the markup percent on cost. Thus, the supplement of 53.8% is 153.8%.

Suppliers—Manufacturers, importers, wholesalers, other resources from whom stores buy merchandise for resale.

Switching Customers—When a salesman cannot close a sale he calls the buyer or department manager or even another salesman whom he introduces as a departmental supervisor, to take over the sale; more prevalent in men's clothing, furniture, or major appliance departments.

Sympathy Strike—A group of workers go on strike because of sympathy with another group who are also on strike.

Syndicate—A group of investment bankers who together underwrite and distribute a new issue of securities or a large block of an outstanding issue.

Syndrome—Combination of signs, symbols, characterizing an abnormality, as the whiplash syndrome.

Synergism—In joint action of agents which when taken together, increase each other's effectiveness.

Synergistic—Working together, synergetic, the cooperative action of two or more ideas, body organs, medicine for increasing the effectiveness of one or more of its properties.

Synthesis—Combination or unification of parts into a whole; as a synthesis of many ideas in planning a merchandise promotion.

Systems Analysis—Recognition of the effect of a change in any part of the system on all the other ingredients of the system.

"Take-Withs"—Merchandise carried from store by customer, expediting delivery and saving delivery expense, particularly signification in branch stores.

Tally(Card or Envelope)—Form on which each salesperson records amount of each transaction; form is sometimes ruled for cash, C.O.D., and charge columns, has column for classification number.

Tape, Punched—Used in sophisticated cash registers to capture price and classification data at point of sale; information is automatically recorded in coded punched paper tape which, in turn, can be processed in computer center.

Tariff—A system of duties levied against goods begin imported into the country.

Tel-Mail—Telephone-order-board and mail-order operation located in the central store, for customers who cannot shop in person at central branch, or regional stores.

Test Promotions—Conducted by store for vendor, presenting a new products, improved products, or selling idea to ascertain reaction of store's customers.

Thirteenth Month—Five selling days before Christmas and New Years.

Ticker Tape—A slip of paper that records within seconds, sales of stock on the large markets.

Tickler—System in which at specific time a flag or notation indicates that merchandise should be reordered.

Tight Money—High interest rates, which influence all facets of business.

Time Utility—Providing goods at the time wanted by consumers.

Top Management—Includes the president, the general manager, vice-presidents, and treasurer of medium and large sized companies.

Total Approach—Utilizing every possible media and promotional avenue to advertise merchandise or service.

Total Automatic Billing—Exclusive use of machine in preparation and mailing store's customer bills.

Total Company—Identifies the aggregate of all units combined in a multi-unit company.

Total Cost of Merchandise Sold—The cost of merchandise sold after adjustment for alteration costs and cash discounts earned, when they exist.

Total Look or Total Concept—Instead of large departments of all kinds of coats, suits, and dresses development of selling areas-commonly called boutiques-appealing to groups of customers, grouped by age, taste, income. Customer no longer has to wander all over store to find things to go with-the-concept, she can find everything in one place.

Total Merchandise Handled—The sum of the beginning inventory plus purchases. It must be calculated at cost and, if the retail method of inventory is used; at retail also.

Total Store—Refers to an individual location only.

Tracer—Personnel in receiving and marking area and traffic department who trace delayed or lost shipments of incoming merchandise; also trace lost deliveries to customers. Also form used in these processes.

Trade Acceptance—A non-interest-bearing bill of exchange or draft covering the sale of goods, drawn by the seller on, and accepted by, the buyer. Its purpose is to put into negotiable form an open account having a short maturity. To be eligible for discount, it must contain the statement that the acceptor's obligation arises out of the purchase of goods from the drawer and it may be accompanied by a record of the purchase. Attempts to popularize the use of trace acceptances having not been generally successful in the United States.

Trade Association—A nonprofit organization, local or national in character, serving common interests of enterprises engaged in the same kind of business.

Trade Discounts—A trade discount is a reduction in price given by a manufacturer to all buyers in a certain class, for example, all wholesalers, all retailers, and so on. Since a different reduction may be given to each group of buyers performing a distinct production or distribution function, trade discounts sometimes are called "functional" discounts. A trade discount is expressed as a percentage reduction or series of percentage reductions, such as 20, 10, and 5 percent, from a manufacturer's quoted base or list price. The list price often is quoted base or list price. The list price often is quoted as a suggested retail price, although it may be higher than the actual retail price. Trade discounts are expected to be adequate to cover normal expenses of the different functional groups and still yield a margin of profit. For example, a manufacturer may give retailers a 30 percent discount, but may give wholesalers a 45 percent one.

Trade Name—The name by which a product is known in commercial circles. It may or may not be registered as a trademark.

Trade Relations—The practices of buyers and of vendors that develop reasonable standards.

Trading Area—Surrounding area from which most of store's trade is drawn, varies by individual store location. Each store, main or branch, needs to know to what extent and from what direction it draws customers; checking automobile license plates in shopping center parking lots, questioning customers who visit store, analyzing charge accounts, etc., will develop this information.

Trading Center—Groups of stores such as downtown shopping centers or neighborhood trading centers.

Trading Instinct—A good trader (buyer) is not one whose primary ambition is to pay less than the price asked; he is one who accurately weighs profit possibilities of sales volume and profit possibilities of each purchase before it is made.

Trading Post—Space on the floor of a stock exchange from which a specified list of stocks can be bought and sold.

Traditional Hours Pattern—Hours during week days, Saturdays, and evening when customer traffic and buying is heavy; therefore, sales and sales supporting personnel must be peaked.

The Marketing Dictionary

Traffic—Number of persons, both prospective and actual customers, who enter store or department.

Traffic Maze—Particularly prevalent in shopping centers with parking facilities for 5,000 or more automobiles and entrances from four directions; and also vehicle traffic in center city, particularly prior to Christmas, Easter and other peak shopping weeks.

Transactions—The number of sales completed during a period, whether cash, charge, or C.O.D., as distinct from value of the sales. Most transaction data are in terms of gross transactions without consideration of the "transaction" involved in returns and allowances. Voided saleschecks, even exchanges, and checks to allow delivery of customer's own goods are excluded.

Transactions per Square Foot—Number of transactions per square foot of selling space are obtained by dividing the number of gross transactions of saleschecks of a department by the average number of square feet the department occupies for selling space.

Transfer Agent—Records changes in ownership following each sale of stock.

Transfer Card—Form used by customers or service shoppers when purchases are made in several departments and a single payment is made.

Transfer In—A purchase from another department or another unit of a chain or branch store system rather than an outside vendor.

Transfer Out—Value of merchandise conveyed to another department or unit of a chain or branch store system. It is not a sale in that it is not a source or profit.

Transit Time—Computed from time merchandise leaves vendor, factory, or warehouse until it arrives at store's receiving stocks.

Trigger Reporting—Immediate reporting on movement (sales) of a specific item, style, color, size or material content.

Trust Company—Financial institutions that specialize in assuming the capacity of trustee for business firms and individuals.

Tube—System of brass tubing in which forced air impels carriers from main selling points to central cashiers or credit authorizers and back to original station.

Turnover—The number of times various assets, such as raw material or other items of inventory, personnel, and the like, are replaced during a stated period, usually a year; the rate of such replacement.

Twig—Small branch store located in community or neighborhood shopping center, generally carrying only women's and children's ready-to-wear and accessories.

"Two for" Plan—A multiple pricing plan in which two articles in a price line or at different price lines are sole jointly for less than the sum of the individual prices. Example: Two $29.95 dresses for $56.

Ultimate Consumer—One who buys and/or uses goods or services to satisfy personal or household wants rather than for resale or use in business, institutional, or industrial operations.

Comment: There seems to be a growing tendency to drop the word "ultimate" from this term. The Committee recommends that this tendency be encouraged. The definition distinguishes sharply between industrial users and ultimate consumers. A firm buying and using an adding machine, a drum of lubricating oil, or a carload of steel billets is an industrial user of those products, not an Ultimate Consumer of them; under the developing usage it is not even a "consumer" of them. A vital difference exists between the purposes motivating the two types of purchases which in turn results in highly significant differences in buying methods, marketing organization, and selling practices.

Uneven Exchange—Merchandise returned by customer or exchange for another article at price different from that of original purchase. Exchange can be in favor of customer (she receives new articles plus refund) or of store (customer pays additional amount of new article purchased).

Unfair Competition—The employment of practices by a seller designed to obtain a larger share of the market by false or misleading advertising, adoption and use of a rival's trademark, discriminatory pricing, selling below costs or dumping, preemptive buying of raw materials, establishing exclusive selling contracts with distributors, securing rebates from suppliers, or adopting any other device that unfairly takes advantage of a competing firm.

Unfair Trade Laws—Endeavor to establish minimum price levels below which goods cannot be sold.

Unfavorable Balance of Trade—When imports exceed exports.

Unisex—A shop or department where outer apparel worn by either men or women is sold.

Unisex Merchandise—Ready-to-wear and accessories designed for both men and women frequently sold in the same department.

Unit Billing—Customer receives single statements, list of articles purchased is posted on detachable strip which store retains for adjustment purposes.

Unit Control—A system of recording vital statistics of stock on hand, on order, and sold for given period; "control" is interpretation of statistics as barometer showing change in customer buying habits; works best when barometer readings are taken frequently and seriously.

Unit Open-to-Buy—The number of pieces of merchandise that are still to be ordered for delivery during a control period. It may be calculated as follows: Maximum in units—(on hand in units and already in order units).

Unit Operator—Personnel in accounts receivable who sort and file sales and credit media in customer's file and are also available for authorizing. Each individual is generally confined to a unit or breakdown of alphabet in cycle billing.

Unsecured Account—A personal account supported by the general credit of the debtor against which no collateral or guaranty is held.

Upgrading—Increase price lines by offering better quality and assortments plus improved visual merchandising in a specific classification of products.

Upgrading Service—Improving service to a store's customers, such as better selling, faster delivery of merchandise.

Upward Expense Trend—Increasing costs of sales and sales-supporting personnel; increased taxes; increased cost of rent, maintenance, operating material, light, heat.

Useful Life—Normal operating life in terms of utility to the owner; said of a fixed asset or a fixed-asset group; the period may be more or less than physical life or any commonly recognized economic life; service life.

Value—Added Tax—A pyramiding form of assessment. At each level of manufacturing and distribution, from the raw material until the finished product is offered to the customer, a tax on the increased value of the product is added.

Value Variable Expenses—Variable expenses varying with the value of the unit or transaction handled, not with the number handled. Thus, if

The Marketing Dictionary

salespeople are paid on a commission basis, selling payroll varies directly with the value of sales. The expense is fixed in percentage, not in dollars.

Variable Expenses—Operating expenses affected by changes in sales volume, increasing as sales increase and decreasing as sales decrease.

Vendor—Manufacturer, wholesaler (jobber), importer, or commission merchant from whom merchandise is purchased.

Vendor Charge backs—Where merchandise is returned to vendor, store submits bill to vendor, frequently accompanied by proof of delivery to vendor.

Vignette—1) Process of deleting background in a photograph used in advertisement; 2) In display, small suggestion of a room setting using complete furnishings but not setting up as a room.

Visual Merchandising—Presentation of merchandise to best selling advantage and for maximum traffic exposure, plus projection of customer "ready-to-buy". Not a display technique but merchandising strategy.

Visual System Stock Control—Method of arranging stock on shelves in piles of equal quantity for quick visual count.

Void—Error which requires writing of new salescheck or re-ringing of amount on cash register; the wrong sales-check or cash register receipt is voided and must be returned to auditing department.

Voluntary Chain—Sponsored by independent wholesalers, and groups of cooperating retailers who band together to take advantage of quantity buying discounts.

Voluntary Self-Regulation—Where an association of manufacturers or other vendors voluntarily develop and police standards of quality and safety prior to regulations voted by national, state or local city governmental legislation.

Wagon Distributor—Make sales and deliveries to retailers from stocks that they carry in their trucks. Also known as a truck distributor.

Walk-Outs—Customers who enter store with acquisitive gleam in eye, walk out dull-eyed and empty-handed. Reasons why vary (absence of merchandise information at point-of-sale, lack of informative labeling, items out of stock due to non-existing basic stock plans, etc. — being fresh out of serpents in garden, i.e., buying temptations).

Wall Street—A street in the heart of the financial district in New York City where the New York Stock Exchange and many brokerage firms and banks are located. The term is commonly used as a synonym for the securities and finance industries.

Want-Slips—A system where salesperson reorders customer's request for merchandise not in stock and tells whether or not a substitute article is sold. The items added to stock on a basis of want slips may make the difference between profit and loss and play an important part in establishing a reputation of leadership and service. Sometimes store makes the form available to customers to fill out and deposit in a box.

Warehouse Manager—Responsible for all warehouse operations for both flagship and branch stores.

Warehouse Receipt—An instrument listing the goods or commodities deposited in a warehouse. This instrument is a receipt for the commodities listed, and for which the warehouse is the bailee. Warehouse receipts may be either non-negotiable receipt specifies to whom the commodities are to be delivered, whereas the negotiable warehouse receipts is made to bearer. Partial releases are permitted under both types of receipts. Title to the commodities on a negotiable warehouse receipt may be transferred from one party to another. Banks will accept a warehouse receipt as collateral for a loan only if the person is a bonded warehouseman. The bank must have protected assurance as to the genuineness of the receipt, and the fact that the commodities pledged are of sound value and fully available as listed in the warehouse receipt.

Warehouse Stock—Merchandise carried in bulk in a remote warehouse for reasons of economy. Some of these stocks are moved into store as department's supply is depleted, but generally saleschecks are filled out and delivery is made directly from warehouse to customer.

Warehousing Unit—A storage area devoted to specific classifications of merchandise, generally remote from flagship store.

Warranty—The act or an instance of warranting assurance; grantee authorization; an express warranty of the quality of goods made by the manufacturer.

Waybill—Shipping form similar manifest or bill of lading, stipulates names of vendor and consignee, shipping instructions, costs, etc.,

Weeding Out—Eliminating slow moving items. Items for which there is very little customer demand. Example: In r-t-w and shoes eliminating extra large and extra small sizes.

White Goods—Refrigerators, deep freezers, automatic dryers, washing machines, stoves, dish washers, all comparatively big ticket items.

Wholesaler Sponsored—Voluntary retail chains sponsored by wholesalers.

Wholesaling—All the marketing functions and activities that involve the sale of goods where the purpose for making the purchase is a business or profit motive. This does not involve sales to the ultimate consumer.

Wildcat Strike—A group of workers go on strike without the official consent of the officers of the union or in violation of the terms of the contract. Also known as an outlaw strike.

Hill Call—Another name applied to lay-away; also applies to purchases which have been paid for in full but which customer will return and pick up.

Window Reader—A sign in a display window containing information on fashion or use of merchandise, including department and location of merchandise.

Working Capital—Difference between the total current assets and total current liabilities.

Workload—The gross number of units of work performed or to be performed in an expense center during a period.

Workrooms—Generally refers to behind-scenes rooms for sales-supporting services such as alterations and repairs.

Workshop—A seminar where the operational problems, objectives, and other mutual areas are discussed by speakers, followed by questions answered by panels.

Written Business—Special orders not reported in daily sales; will be reported when merchandise arrives from vendor and is delivered.

Yield—Also known as return. The dividends or interest paid by a company expressed as a percentage of the current price or, if you own the security, of the price you originally paid.

Youth Market—Women, men under 25 years of age, including babies, children, subteens, teens, young men and women primarily interested in the new, different, unusual; often in contrast to the tastes of members of older generations, and sometimes in heated opposition.

The Marketing Dictionary

Zone Pricing—In some industries, freight rates are averaged for sections of the country and every buyer in each zone is charged the same freight rate. Throughout a section of the country, such as the Southwest, every buyer would be billed the same freight charge. Some buyers would thus pay a little above actual rates and some a little below. Every buyer in the zone, however, would have the same delivered cost at his place of business. Here the seller would have to pay the carrier and bill the buyer. A wide variety of manufactured food products, for example, are marketed by this system.